The Adventures of Huckleberry Finn

A play

Adapted by **Matthew Francis**

From the novel by Mark Twain

Samuel French — London
New York - Toronto - Hollywood

Please see page vi for further copyright information

THE ADVENTURES OF HUCKLEBERRY FINN

First presented at the Greenwich Theatre, London, on 6th
December 1996, with the following cast:

Huckleberry Finn	Daniel Newman
Jim	Clive Llewellyn

St Petersburg, Missouri

Miss Watson	Lois Baxter
The Widow Douglas	Ruth Arnold
Tom Sawyer	Andrew Muir
Judge Thatcher	Ray Llewellyn
Pap	Nathan Osgood
Pike	Roger Moss
Judith Loftus	Lois Baxter

On the Raft

Preacher	David Killick
Mr Smith	Ray Llewellyn

The Grangerfords and the Shepherdsons

Colonel Grangerford	David Killick
Ma Grangerford	Lois Baxter
Bob Grangerford	Ian Gelder
Tom Grangerford	Nathan Osgood
Sophia Grangerford	Ruth Arnold
Charlotte Grangerford	Roger Moss
Buck Grangerford	Andrew Muir
Harney Shepherdson	Roger Moss

On the Mississippi Again

The King	David Killick
The Duke	Ian Gelder

Wilks and Sherburn

Peter Wilks	Ray Llewellyn
Sherburn	Nathan Osgood
Mary-Jane Wilks	Lois Baxter

Susan Wilks	Ruth Arnold
Judge Bell	Roger Moss
Doctor Robinson	Nathan Osgood
Abner Shackleford	Andrew Muir
Harvey Wilks	Ray Llewellyn
William Wilks	Roger Moss

Other parts played by members of the company

Directed by Matthew Francis
Designed by Russell Craig
Lighting designed by Howard Harrison
Music by Mia Soteriou
Sound designed by Ed Brimley
Choreography by Andrew George
Assistant Director Philip Wilson
University of South Florida placements:
Julian Fletcher, Erica Jensen

Students involved in the original USF workshops were:
Alan Fessenden, Julian Fletcher, D. Christian Gottshall,
Missy Hicks, Erica Jensen, Vince Lasala, Jason Quinn,
Monica Reagan, Jane Robinson, Bridget Roney and
Heather Smith

CHARACTERS

Huckleberry Finn
Jim
Miss Watson
The Widow Douglas
Tom Sawyer
Judge Thatcher
Pap
Pike
Judith Loftus
Preacher
Mr Smith
Colonel Grangerford
Ma Grangerford
Bob Grangerford
Tom Grangerford
Sophia Grangerford
Charlotte Grangerford
Buck Grangerford
Harney Shepherdson
The King
The Duke
Peter Wilks
Sherburn
Mary-Jane Wilks
Susan Wilks
Judge Bell
Doctor Robinson
Abner Shackleford
Harvey Wilks
William Wilks

Other parts played by members of the Company

The action takes place in various interior and exterior settings

Time — nineteenth century

This adaptation was inspired by a series of workshops
on *Huckleberry Finn* undertaken by Matthew Francis
with students from the Department of Theatre at
The University of South Florida.

PRODUCTION NOTES

DESIGN

It is essential that the story of the play moves along at a good pace. A composite set — on which swift changes of light can suggest new locations — is preferable to a series of sets that take valuable time to position and therefore slow up the action. At Greenwich, many of the props stayed on stage as set-dressing throughout the play — the canoe, assorted cases, chairs, tables, ropes, the pole for the raft, even items of costume. This speeded transitions, suggesting the clutter of memory, and giving an "adventure playground" feel to the production which suits the style of the story.

CAST SIZE

We presented the play with ten actors. There is no reason why this number should not be increased substantially. Actors playing only one or two smaller roles could be an important part of the ensemble. A production with twenty-five or more performers could field a whole crowd of Blackhats at the top of the show, a townful of people to protest at Huck's abduction by Pap, forestsfuls of sound effects, a posse of bounty hunters, a big extended family for the Grangerfords and so on.

TONE

Huck's life on the river is an escape from the tough world on shore. Many of the characters he encounters there have a nightmare quality: Pap (obviously), Pike, Sherburn, and the Preacher. But even Miss Watson, The Duke, The King and Colonel Grangerford can be sinister or frightening as well as flamboyant/eccentric/amusing. Huck and Jim ricochet between these characters — their lives and freedom constantly in danger. At times their encounters with villains, rascals, or madmen are hilariously funny, but the context is often grotesque and the outcome either potentially or actually horrific.

MUSIC

There is an original score for this version of *Huckleberry Finn*. It was composed by Mia Soteriou and is available on DAT or cassette from RACHEL DANIELS at LONDON MANAGEMENT, 2-4 Noel Street, London W1V 3RB (0171 287 9000). Sheet music for the Grangerford song is also available.

Publisher's note: Arkansas has been spelt phonetically in this Edition.

Other plays by Matthew Francis published by
Samuel French Ltd:

Northanger Abbey
The Prisoner of Zenda
A Tale of Two Cities

This adaptation is dedicated to my godsons
Benjamin Sheinwald
and
Alfie Brown
with love and luck
for the big river.

ACT I

Night Terrors

A big old-fashioned bed with crisp old-fashioned bedclothes; high off the ground, uncomfortable. There are books on a table and coats hanging on the wall

Huckleberry (Huck) is asleep in the bed but wakes suddenly. The Lights snap up as he wakes. He's startled, we're startled

Huck Tom and me found the money! Where Injun Joe hid it. Under that rock. But I don't want it no more. They can have it. The six thousand dollars. *I don't want it!* Deadwood earnest! They can keep it. Bein' rich ain't what it's cracked up to be. It's just worry and worry and sweat and sweat. I got to wear them blamed clothes that just smothers me ... just *smothers* me ...

Jim comes forward from the shadows. Hushes him. Lies him down again and sings a lullaby to Huck

Jim (*singing*)　　Hush little baby, don't you cry;
　　　　　　　　　　Down by the river, the morning come by —
　　　　　　　　　　And one of these mornings you're gonna be free,
　　　　　　　　　　Big river run slow, but out to the sea.

Jim slips away

But immediately, the shadows in the room begin to dance and stir. Huck grows restless again

Huck No. Stop it. You leave me alone. *Go away!*

A figure appears from behind the bed: he wears ragged clothes and an old black hat with the top caved in

Blackhat 1(Pap) This is the tale of Huckleberry Finn ...

Huck "wakes" into the dream

Huck What do you want from me? You left us! I ain't goin' nowhere with
you no more!

Another figure (Blackhat 2) melts up through the floor

Blackhat 2 Huckleberry Finn! Born April 25th 1835!
Huck They said we could keep the money! But you can have it! Tom and
me found it in the robbers' cave — but you can have it!

A third figure (Blackhat 3) comes through the window

Blackhat 3 Born 25th April 1835, and raised in St Petersburg, Missouri.

*The three work at untidying the room: pulling at the bedding, and juggling
with Huck's books*

Huck Stop it! *Stop it!* I'm about ready to quit. I'll make a break for it!

He climbs up on to the roof of the bedroom

Another Blackhat (4) is there

Blackhat 4 Raised in St Petersburg — a pauper and a heathen.
Huck Stop that! I didn't do it! Whatever it was — *I didn't do it!*
Blackhat 2 Fluttering with rags, sleeping on doorsteps ...
Huck You left me there, you left us all! You didn't care!
Blackhat 1 But now a rich pup in a rich pup's bed!
Huck I hate it here! I hate it hate it *hate it!*
Blackhat 1 A rich pup in a rich pup's bed ...
Blackhat 4 ... but still the son of the town drunkard!
Huck Go away from here. I'm not coming with you. And don't you make
me!
Blackhats The tale of Huckleberry Finn. Born April 25th 1835. Raised in
St Petersburg, Missouri. *Son of the town drunkard.*

Blackhat 1 (Pap) drives a knife into the wall of the room

Huck *Pap!*

SCENE 2

Life with the Widow

*Miss Watson and the Widow Douglas appear at the door with a lamp. They
stand and survey the chaos*

The Blackhats freeze, the shadows settle

Miss Watson Huckleberry Finn!
Widow Huckleberry dear!

And the Blackhats are gone

During the following, the Widow and Huck tidy up a little

Miss Watson What is this caterwauling?
Widow You were making such a noise, dear.
Miss Watson *And what is this mess?*
Huck I wus in a dream.
Miss Watson When you made the mess?
Huck When I made the noise.
Miss Watson Look at these clothes!
Widow And look at the floor!
Miss Watson And look at the bed!
Widow Was it a nightmare?
Miss Watson Can't you sleep a little neater?
Widow It must've been a bad one. You poor dear.
Miss Watson Don't coddle the boy!
Widow I'm not coddling him. Just giving him a little good attention.
Huck I'm all right. I'm just fine.
Widow Now you lie down ——
Miss Watson Screaming out ——
Widow — and make yourself comfy ——
Miss Watson — wakin' all the neighbours ...
Widow — and don't you dream no more.
Huck I thought I saw ... I thought that p'raps ...
Miss Watson Perhaps you thought you saw the devil's ferryman, bringin'
his old master into heads full of wickedness and sin.
Huck I thought I saw my Pap.
Widow Perhaps we should say a prayer.
Huck I said my prayers.
Miss Watson Perhaps you did *not.*

Widow Dear Lord ——
Miss Watson Dear Lord ——
Huck Dear Lord ——
Miss Watson You sit up when you say your prayers. You show some respect!
Huck You just told me to lie down!
Miss Watson Dear Lord!
Huck Dear Lord!
Widow Now don't scrunch up like that: sit up straight!
Miss Watson Dear Lord. If I should die tonight, please take my soul and carry it to heaven.
Huck Please tell me, Mrs Douglas, what is heaven?
Miss Watson Huckleberry Finn! What a question to ask!
Widow (*quickly*) It's where the good Lord lives with his angels and all the good souls he has saved from eternal damnation.
Huck And what goes on in this heaven?
Widow Why, singin', and praisin' the Lord, and playin' upon harps ...
Huck And will Miss Watson be goin' there?
Widow Why surely.
Huck Well, I'm not goin' where she's goin' — so I won't try for it!
Miss Watson *Huckleberry Finn, you is the worst and wickedest boy on the face of God's earth*!
Widow You say you're sorry to my sister.
Miss Watson You and me will see each other in the morning, Huckleberry Finn! You and me will have a talk you won't forget.
Huck Will Tom Sawyer go to heaven do you think?
Miss Watson Not by a considerable sight! He's heading for the other place.
Huck Well — I hope I'll be there to see him.
Miss Watson *There*! That's the devil speaking.
Widow How could you, Huckleberry? How could you say such a thing?
Huck Oh, please Miss Douglas — don't cry. I didn't mean you no harm.
Miss Watson Leave the boy alone. I'll deal with him in the morning!
Widow Oh Huckleberry ——
Miss Watson Wicked, wicked boy ——
Widow — what's to become of you ——
Miss Watson — what's to be done with you ——
Widow My poor, poor boy.
Miss Watson — I'll deal with him in the morning.

Miss Watson and the Widow are gone, taking the warm glow of lamplight with them

Tom Sawyer

Shadows and darkness. Night noises from outside. Moonlight through the window

Huck Well — I should say I wasn't much for sleepin' after all that. So I tried to sit by the window and think of something cheerful. But it weren't no use. The stars were shining, and the leaves rustlin' in the woods, ever so mournful; and I heard an owl away off, who-whoin' about somebody that was goin' to die, and the wind was tryin' to whisper something to me, and I couldn't make out what it was, and so it made the cold shivers run over me. I got so downhearted and scared, I did wish I had some company. I heard a twig snap down amongst the trees. Something was stirring.
Tom's Voice Huckleberry ...
Huck (*picking up a stick*) Get away!
Tom's Voice *Huckleberry* ...
Huck I told you before, I'm not comin' with you ...
Tom's Voice *Huckleberry Finn!*
Huck Why don't you just go away and stay away!

Tom leaps in through the window, sweeps his hat off and bows elegantly

Tom It's only me.
Huck Tom! Tom Sawyer!
Tom The castle wall was high, but I made good use of the vines and such like.
Huck You scared me half to death!
Tom Put that stick down — you don't look friendly. It's me — *Tom.*
Huck Well, I can see it's you *now.*
Huck }
Tom } (*together; making their secret sign*) *Fox — Wolf — Bear!*
Tom You seem a little edgy, Huck.
Huck I — I thought you was my Pap.
Tom Oh, Huckleberry —
Huck I guess I bin dreamin' ...
Tom I ain't no ghost —
Huck It seemed like he was here.
Tom The dead don't walk on a night full o' moonshine.
Huck What do you mean — the dead?
Tom Well ain't you heard?
Huck Heard what?
Tom About your father — about your Pap. It was me that found him. I

thought it was a log. But then I pushed at it and saw it was a man. Lying in the water. A dead man. I rode back to town and spread the word, then led the people down to where the body was. I knew it was your Pap. Same size, same clothes, same hair —uncommon long.

Huck (*after a moment*) Did you git a look at his face?

Tom I couldn't make nothin' of the face. It had been in the water so long. It warn't much like a face at all. He was just floating on his back and staring up to heaven.

Huck That weren't my Pap. That weren't a man at all.

Tom Now, Huck. I saw him — arms and legs and head. It weren't no catfish!

Huck It were a woman.

Tom A woman!

Huck I thought you would'a known. A drownded man don't float on his back, but on his face. That were a woman dressed in a man's clothes.

Tom Why Huckleberry Finn, that's a proper thing to know.

Huck So he'll turn up again.

Tom I need that kind o' learning in my gang.

Huck (*immediately interested*) Your gang?

There is a sudden knock at the door

The boys freeze

Who's there?

Jim (*off*) Only me, Honey.

Huck (*to Tom*) It's Jim! He mustn't find you here. It's best. You gotta hide!

Tom Is there a secret panel in the wall, perhaps? Princes go in and out of castles every day through such a thing.

Huck Not that I know.

Jim (*off*) Huck? *Huck?*

Huck Under the bed!

Tom (*long-suffering*) Well, it's not what they do in books, but I suppose ...

Huck Quick!

Tom Huck! Knock three times when the danger is past.

And Tom disappears from sight under the bed

Huck (*to the audience*) Jim was Miss Watson's slave.

Jim (*off*) Huck! Is you all right?

Huck I had told him Pap was in my mind again ... (*Opening the door*) Jim! What is it?

Jim enters the room

Jim I heard de row. I heard d'ole missus peckin' at you an' I heard her crash
de door and pray real loud for very near a half an hour ...
Huck I had a dream I guess ...
Jim Another like de last?
Huck It seemed like Pap was back again.
Jim Come here, Huck. (*Beat*) Your ole father don't know yit what he's a
goin' to do. Sometimes he spec he'll keep away, en den agin he spec he'll
come. De bes' way is to res' easy and let de ole man take his own way.
Dey's two angels hoverin' roun' 'bout him. One of dem is bright and shiny,
and d'other one is dark. De bright one gits him to go right a little while, den
de dark one sail in an' bust it all up. But you is all right. You goin' to have
considerable trouble in your life, and considerable joy. First one jump out
at you, and den de oder.

*As he says this, Tom rises up from behind him, covered in a sheet from the
bed*

First one creep up on you, but den de oder throw his arms around you.

Tom obliges with a demonstration

Tom I am de bright angel, Honey! This is your happy day!
Jim Don't hurt me! Don't come near me! I lived a good life: I's goin' to the
good place when I die.

Tom chases Jim round the room, then whips off the sheet

Tom Only me, Honey.
Jim Why, may the Lord forgive you, Tom Sawyer. Sneakin' up on me. Who
is you to go scarin' a soul like that?
Tom Why, Jim, I is the Prince of Araby, and genies do whatever I might say,
and bring me chewin' gum and diamonds.
Jim Don't you mock de oder world! I got a quarter roun' my neck the divil
lef' me — tole me it could cure any poor soul, tole me it could fetch down
witches if I need dem ...
Tom Then you can join our gang and waltz down witches when we need 'em;
and you, Huck, can be my right-hand man, and help us with the dead
bodies. We'll need the bravest weapons and the sharpest knives. What
have you got, Huck?
Huck The Persian spear that used to be a handle for the Widow's broom ...
Tom (*seeing the knife Pap left in the wall of the room*) But you is better armed
than most I see ...
Huck I had a blund'rbuss, but Jim borrowed it for a gate post in the yard.

Tom But the knife, Huck. Where did you get the knife?

Huck I ain't got no knife.

Tom Not a silver-handled fella with a rope worked on the pommel and a brace o' notches in the blade?

Huck What are you talkin' about?

Tom Kinda rough. Could be a pirate's. Moose head on the side.

Huck It's my Pap's. What do you know about it, Tom Sawyer? Where you seen that knife? Where you seen it, Tom?

Tom Why it's here. As if you didn't know.

Huck I knew it weren't no dream. I knew that he'd be back!

Jim I'll tell the missus.

Tom No!

Huck No! No. I reckon he had to come some time or other. It's just as you said, Jim.

Jim and Tom vanish. Pap steps out from behind the coats on the wall

Pap!

Pap (*dangerous, absurd*) You think you're a good deal of a big-bug, don't you?

Huck (*carefully*) Maybe I am, maybe I ain't.

Pap (*the bully*) Don't give me none of your lip. You've put on considerable many frills since I been away. I'll take you down a peg before I get done with you. You're educated too, they say — can read and write. You think you're better than your father now, because he can't? I'll take it out of you. Who told you you might meddle with such highfalutin' foolishness, hey? Who told you you could?

Huck The Widow.

Pap I'll learn her how to meddle. And looky here — you drop that school, you hear? Your mother couldn't read — no, and she couldn't write neither, before she died. *I* can't. None of the family couldn't before they died. (*Picking up a book*) Say — lemme hear you read.

Huck "As for his clothes — just rags, that was all. The boot on one foot was busted, and two of his toes stuck through. His hair was all tangled up like a mat and his face was filthy ..."

Pap (*smashing the book out of Huck's hand*) It's so. You can do it. I'll lay for you, my smarty. And if I catch you about that school, I'll tan you real good. (*He stops, looks at Huck, giggles*) Ain't you a sweet-scented dandy, though? A bed, and bedclothes; and a lookin'-glass; and a piece of carpet on the floor ... and your own father got to sleep with the hogs in the tanyard. I never seen such a son. (*A beat*) They say you're rich. How's that?

Huck They lie. That's how.

Pap Looky here — mind how you talk to me; I'm a-standin' about all I can stand now — so don't give me no sass. I've been in town two days, and I ain't heard nothing but about you being rich. They say you found gold, boy, hidden in a cave by the river. Ain't you the lucky one ...

Huck I ain't got no money.

Pap It's a lie. Judge Thatcher's got it. And you're goin' to git it for me!

Huck I ain't got no money — I tell you. You ask Judge Thatcher — he'll tell you the same.

Pap I'll make him give it over. You and me — we're goin' to work on that. You're my boy. They can't keep you here. You're my nat'ral son. (*A beat*) That's why I come. To git you. You and me — we goin' to be a family once again.

SCENE 4

Kidnapped!

Music. The Lights shift and change to suggest the violent abduction

Pap grabs Huck and drags him, kicking and struggling, from the room

Huck calls out to Jim, who arrives just too late to save him

The Widow and Miss Watson call after Pap and Huck as they make a journey up and over the set (Others could also call)

Widow (*off*) The father's taken him. My boy. Huckleberry!

Miss Watson (*off*) The devil came for the devil's child!

Widow (*off*) We'll go to court for him.

Pap (*furious*) I'll see you there! The boy's my child. His money's mine by rights. I'll have it yet!

Widow (*off*) The boy was happy here. This was a home for him — the first he'd known: simple and clean ... school in the morning, prayers when he went to bed.

Huck I didn't like that so well neither — havin' to wash and eat on a plate and comb up and go to bed and get up reg'lar.

Judge (*off*) A drunkard! A villain and a drunkard! A monument of rags and dirt. Profane when he's sober, savage when he's drunk!

Miss Watson (*off*) The devil came for the devil's child!

Pap No more school, no more fancy ways. I'll show y'all who Huck Finn's boss is! Keep your distance now!

They have arrived at Pap's cabin in the woods. There is a straw mattress on the floor, a stove, a barrel, some bottles. No window; one door

Huck (*to the audience*) He took me up the river about three miles — and crossed over to a cabin on the Illinois shore, where the timber was so thick, you couldn't find it if you didn't know where it was.

Pap And if they come to git you, well — I know a place that's six or seven mile off — I'll stow you there and they'll hunt till they drop — but they won't find you.

Huck They'll come.

Pap Git down and make some supper. You light the fire. Now it's time for you to work, boy. You bin poisoned by their fancy ways too long.

Huck The law'll come and git me.

Pap The law? You think I give a skunk's hide for the law. Why — here's the law a-standin' ready to take a man's son away from him — a man's own son, which he had all the trouble and all the anxiety and all the expense of raising — What do you say to *that*?

Huck I don't say nothin', sir. I ain't the law. I don't know the law ...

Pap The law takes a man worth six thousand dollars and upards, and jams him into an old trap of a cabin like this, and lets him go round in clothes that ain't fitten for a hog. You call that *gov'ment*?

Huck I don't call it nothin'. The gov'ment don't keep me here.

Pap I tell you what, boy — I may get my money in the end, but the Widow'll go to court for *you*. And folks think that she'll win ...

Huck I won't go back there ...

Pap (*violently*) You can go to blazes. For two cents I'd leave you and this blamed country for good. There was a free nigger in town — from Ohio. He had on the whitest shirt you ever see, and the shiniest hat, and he had a gold watch and a chain, and a silver-headed cane — the awfullest ole gray-headed nabob in the state. They said he was a p'fessor in a college. They said he could *vote*! What is this country a'comin' to? Why ain't this nigger put up at auction and sold? Why? *Why*?

Huck There ain't no slavery in Ohio. He can come and go.

Pap I'll give you come and go. I'll tan your hide. Come here, God dammit. I'm your father — you come here.

Pap stumbles, falls over, hurts himself, screams out

Give me the whiskey, boy, you bring it here. I've got enough for all the drunks in town and one delirium tremens. Give it to me, give it to me!

Huck gives him the whiskey

Pap drinks and drinks

Huck circles him, watching. Pap is now in a state of extreme intoxication. He half sings a song, muttering to himself

Huck (*over this*) I won't stay here no more. I'm leavin' you. If I get through tonight, I'll go tomorrow. I know how. You just lie down. You go to sleep. It's easy. Just lie down. I'll keep as quiet as a mouse. I won't be no bother — just go to sleep, rest up — and then go back to town. I've got a plan Tom Sawyer would be proud of ...

Pap fades into unconsciousness. Huck lies down

SCENE 5

Delirium Tremens

Abruptly, frighteningly, Pap sits up; raving

Huck springs into a corner

Pap Snakes! No — *No — Get them off*! — Get them off o' me! — Get off, get off! Snakes ... all over ... on my legs, my poor legs ... snakes crawling over my legs ... I can't shift 'em... They'll kill me — kill me — kill me ...
Huck There ain't no snakes!
Pap Argh! They're on my face! — bitten, bitten — here — on my cheek — on my cheek! Take him off, take him off, take him off, take him off, take him off *take him off* me! This one — this one on my neck. Please, *please* ... please ...
Huck There ain't no snakes!
Pap Devils — devils — pulling me down — down into hell — deeper than hell — into the snakes ... pulling me down ...

He is suddenly still: horrified, listening

Tramp, tramp, tramp; that's the dead; tramp — tramp — tramp; they're coming after me; but I won't go! Oh they're here! — Don't touch me — don't! Hands off — they're cold — let go — oh, let a poor devil alone!

He whimpers and cries and begs. Then he sees Huck

You. You. The angel of death. I see you now. I'll kill you, kill you dead — then you won't come for me no more. I'll kill *you* — yes — kill the angel of death afore *he* kills *me*! Kill the angel of death ...
Huck I ain't no angel! It's me! Huckleberry Finn! Keep away. You're drunk and dreamin'.

Pap gives an awful screechy laugh

Pap Damn you, damn you. You're dead. Come here. Don't fly away. I have to kill you, see, so you won't come back for me again. Goddam — my legs — my legs won't move, won't stir. Tired now ... tired out. I'll rest a minute, then I'll kill you ... kill you later ... kill you ...

And he subsides: out cold. From far away — a note of music, a note of hope, of possibility

Huck It came for me. Yesterday — when I was fishin'. A beauty, too: ten foot. Riding high in the water like a duck. Pap was in the shanty still. I swam out to it, climbed in, brought her ashore. It was a *drift canoe*. I hid her good. (*He lies down to sleep*)

A cock crows. Light comes

Pap starts awake

Pap What time is it? Blamed thing ... I gotta go — I'm meetin' the lawyer. He'll get my money for me. You — you clear this place, y'hear? Why don't you do suthin' for a change. I'll lock y'in while I'm away. I know you, boy. Need to lock you in ...

He stumbles out, locking the door

SCENE 6

Escape

Music again, and voices from all over the set. They "remind" Huck about the stages of his plan

He acts it out, taking equipment to the canoe, shooting a pig and so on

Voice The plan, Huckleberry!
Voice You go to work, boy!
Voice The secret plan!

Huck pulls at a piece of the wall, reveals a hole

Voice Take everything!
Voice The whiskey and the bacon ——
Voice The bucket and the tin cup ——
Voice The skillet and the coffee pot ——

Voice The fish lines and the blankets ——
Voice And the gun!
Voice Now put 'em in the boat!
Voice Hurry! It's nearly three o'clock!
Voice Now — take the gun out the back ——
Voice Something'll come along ——
Voice One o' the wild pigs ——
Voice Take care! Don't miss!

The sound of a shot

Voice Nice work, boy!
Voice Hurry, boy, hurry — it's getting on for five!
Voice Go back and get the pig!
Voice Carry him, carry him; don't drag him —- lay him on the ground to bleed —
Voice Then drag him down to the river —
Voice Makin' a good trail of blood, so no-one can miss it!
Voice Now — throw him in!
Voice Now — go get the axe, and wipe it with blood ... pull out a bundle of your hair. Stick it to the blood ——
Voice And leave it on the ground!
Voice Now — take the cornmeal — it's in the cabin, by the stove!
Voice Bring it outside!
Voice Trail it away across the grass!
Voice Through the willows east of the cabin ——
Voice Down to the Five Mile lake! It's nearly dark —- he'll soon be back!
Voice *Now*!
All *The canoe*!

Music bursts out here

The Company move round Huck; and lift both him and the canoe into the air

Huck And they'll follow the track of blood to the shore and drag the river for me — And they'll follow the track of meal to the lake to find the robbers that killed me — And they'll hunt the river for my dead carcass — And when they've done — they won't bother no more about Huckleberry Finn! Not Pap, or the Widow, or Miss Watson: And I'll be free. *Free*!

The music swells

SCENE 7

Jackson's Island

Huck I didn't lose no more time. The next minute I was a' spinnin' away soft but quick in the shade of the bank. I came to Jackson's Island, about two mile and a half downstream: big and dark and solid — like a steamboat without any lights. I run the canoe into a deep dent in the bank that I knows about. When I made fast — nobody coulda' seen the canoe from the outside.

The Company set the canoe down and melt away. Huck begins to unload the canoe, and set up camp

Evening on the river. Echoey sounds

Voices from over the water

Voice 1 Hey — aah!
Huck (*startled*) What's that?
Voice 1 Stern oars there! Heave her head to starboard!
Huck (*relieved*) Lumber raft. A mile upstream.
Voice 2 (*singing*)   There was a woman in our town,
                 In our town did dwell —
                 She loved her husband dear — i — lee —
                 But another man twice as well ...

The sound of a loud, echoey boom, out on the river

Huck Next evenin' I watched the ferry boat go by. They was firing cannon over the water, tryin' to make my carcass come to the top ——

Another loud boom

  'Most everyone was on the boat ...

Voices from the dark are heard across the water

Widow He was like a son ...
Pap And if he's dead — the money comes to me!
Judge I'm mighty interested to hear you say so, Mr Finn ...
Tom Of course — the body will be floatin' face down ...
Miss Watson He goes to a better place — if the good Lord will have him ...

A final "boom"

During the following, Jim enters

Huck I knowed I was all right now. Nobody else would come a-huntin' after me. But, by and by, I got sort of lonesome, and so I went and set on the bank and listened to the currents washin' along, and counted the stars and the drift logs and the rafts that came down ... and then I went to bed. There ain't no better way to put in time when you're lonesome; you can't stay so, you soon get over it. And so it was for three nights ...

SCENE 8

Jim

Beat. Then — panic! Huck leaps to his feet

Huck Why, *Jim*!

Jim (*terrified*) Doan hurt me — don't! I hain't ever done no harm to a ghos'. I awluz liked dead people, en done all I could for 'em. You go en git in de river agin, where you b'longs, en doan do nuffin to ole Jim, 'at 'uz awluz yo fren' ...

Huck I ain't dead, Jim!

Jim Blame you chile — don't you know nuffin 'tall? You is dead! De bad man killed yourself and threw yo' body in de river!

Huck Jim — *No*!

Jim An' all de ladies and gen'l'men go over to see de place you's killed, an' de judge say you is killed, and de Widder say you's killed ....

Huck Jim — listen!

Jim Dere ain't no point in goin' furder! You is dead, Honey. And now I's talkin' to a ghos' and de divil'll surely come f'me ...

Huck Jim! *Jim*! I ain't dead — I'm alive — I escaped — (*in one breath*) I sawed a hole in the wall and found a boat and killed a pig and made a trail o'blood to the river an' a trail o' corn to the lake and I stuck my hair to the blade of the axe and took the cup and the blankets and the bacon and the sugar and the skillet and the fish-lines and the whiskey and the bucket and the gun and I threw the pig in the river and I put the wood back in the hole and I covered my tracks and I put things in the boat and spun the boat downstream and I set up camp here and I made everyone think I was dead and it wuz all my plan and everybody thinks I *am* dead. *Even you*!

Jim (*after a suitable beat*) Why, you *rapscallion*. De Widder goana be dat *mad* wid you.

Huck But that ain't nothin' to what she'll be with you. I'm not afraid of you tellin' folk where I am. How d'*you* come to be here, Jim?

Jim Maybe I better not tell.

Huck Why?

Jim Well, dey's reasons. But you wouldn't tell on me?

Huck Blamed if I would, Jim!

Jim Well — I b'lieve you, Huck. I — I run off.

Huck (*amazed*) Jim!

Jim (*alarmed*) You said you wouldn't tell!

Huck (*a big moment for Huck*) Well, I did. I did. I said I wouldn't and I'll stick to it. Honest injun I will. People can call me a low-down abolitionist and despise me for keepin' mum — but that don't make no difference. So now — let's know all about it!

Jim Well, you see, it uz dis way. I noticed dey wuz a slave-trader roun' de place considerable, lately, and I begun to git oneasy. Well — de night before you wuz killed — I creeps to de do' pooty late, en I hear dis man talkin' wid de ole missus …

The light shifts to the Widow's room which "takes over" from the island scene

Widow But you can't sell him! Esther! How would we manage?

Pike But the purchaser is more than generous.

Miss Watson Mr Pike — tell Mrs Douglas the terms.

Pike My client is a conn'oser. He is a master of his trade. This slave ——

Widow His name is *Jim* …

Pike — this slave is worth eight hundred dollars to him.

Miss Watson Eight hundred dollars, Martha. Think of that.

Widow Who *is* the purchaser?

Pike A gentleman of substance. Noble. Particular. Ask any man in Arkansaw — he'll tell you. Colonel Sherburn has a reputation.

Widow Selling him down the river … why — he's a piece of us.

Miss Watson Come back tomorrow, Mr Pike — and bring your gold!

The lights focus back to Jim and Huck

Jim I lit out mighty quick, I tell you. I hid by de sho' to wait for ev'rybody to go 'way, an' when it came dark, I tuck out up de river road. I'd made up my mind — a raf' is what I's after. It doan make no track. I saw a piece o' one come roun' de p'int, so I swam out agin de current an' clumb up on her en laid down on de planks. I got cau't in de snags back o' dis island, but brought her roun' an' made her fast. I bin here two days now.

Huck Welcome to the island, Jim! It's real nice here. I wouldn't want to be
nowhere else — nor with no-one else neither!
Jim Why, Huck — dat's jus' how I look on it 'n all!
Huck You must be most starved, ain't you?
Jim I reckon I could eat a hoss. I tink I could!

Music

*Activity. Hucks lights a fire; Jim catches a huge catfish which both of them
struggle to land, before it gets the better of them. They fall back, laughing*

The light shifts to the Widow's room which "takes over" again

Pike (*furious*) Gone!
Miss Watson But we've hunted high and low ...
Pike Colonel Sherburn will be most unhappy!
Miss Watson But Jim has never given any trouble. He's the best of servants.
Pike Not the best of slaves. You'll offer a reward.
Miss Watson How much?
Pike Three hundred dollars. We'll set that off against the purchase price.
Miss Watson Where can he be?
Pike He won't git far. I'll track him down. He's big. I'll find that boy.
Miss Watson Don't harm him! Promise me — you'll not harm him!
Pike Harm him? But he's a runaway. A runaway, Miss Watson. Way beyond
the law ...

Pike and Miss Watson go

Scene 9

Snakes Alive

The following evening on the island

Huck I killed a snake this mornin', Jim. Right here — right in our camp! A
beauty!
Jim What you do wid it?
Huck (*smiling*) Hidden it.
Jim Where?
Huck Nearby.
Jim *You git rid o' dat ting, you hear me?* Dat is de worse luck — touch a dead
snake! Worse still — keep 'n.
Huck But our luck's in! It's here, Jim! We got out.

Jim (*irritated*) Never you mind, Honey, never you mind. And don't you git too peart. Dese tings come round. You kep dat snake, an' dat snake fetch bad luck. I tell you it's a comin'!

Huck I'm sorry, Jim —

Jim I tell you it's a-comin', an' dere ain't no way we kin slide by it!

Huck *Jim* — I'll show you where !

Jim (*getting under his blanket*) I's goan sleep now. In the mornin' — take de ting — an' troe it in de river ——

Huck *Jim* — *it's there*!

Jim — an' den us done wid it!

Huck *Under your blanket*!

Jim Ahh! It bit me, Huck — *de blame ting bit me*!

Huck Jim, it's *dead*. It can't bite you ——

Jim *Don't you know nuthin'*? De dead snake wife come to find him, an' curl up roun' his body! *She* de one dat bite! Look — *look*! Dere, dere! Huck — kill de ting now — dere on de ground — *dere*!

Huck attacks the snake with a stick. (Production note: if the stick and blanket are set carefully, — a rubber snake can be attached to the end of the stick with magician's wire, then the snake really dances when Huck beats it to death)

Huck My Lord, I'm sorry, Jim, I'm sorry. Look — it's dead — can't bite you again — I'm sorry, Jim. Where'd it git you, Jim?

Jim Here on de heel. Git me da whiskey, Huck — I gotta drink it all — dat'll help it — yer Pap's whiskey, Huck!

Huck Whiskey, whiskey — here Jim — here y'are ... all o' Pap's whiskey...

Jim Oh Lord, oh Lord — dis whiskey — *Hi — Ahh — Oh oh oh oh* — drink it down and drive de pison out ——

Huck I'll go git help. I'll go back to St Pete. Any woman got the remedy in her home. I'll git it for you — Jim — I'll go ...

Jim Dey'll know you, boy, dey'll take you back — *Aieee* — I'll git tro' dis ... oh my Lord, de whiskey, de whiskey ...

Huck I want to go — I want to go — and they won't git me. I got a plan — *I got a plan*! I'll do exactly what Tom Sawyer would've done. *Go in disguise*! He showed me how. I'll steal somethin' from a clothes line! *Jim* — lie back. Lie back an' you'll be fine ... lie back!

Huck races away

SCENE 10

A Reward

A light picks up the figure of Pike, addressing a crowd

Pike Three hundred dollars for the murderin' slave. Three hundred dollars
for the slave — alive: I want him alive. He's out there, watchin', waitin'.
Whose child will he murder next — your little Jane, your little Johnny?
He's still in Jefferson County, gentlemen. Make yourself rich, and our poor
children safe. Arrest the slave. And let the ab'litionists take note — a slave
will live and die a slave in this state. Scour the country. Jim is the murderer's
name. Find him and bring him in. Bring him to *me*!

Lights out on Pike, and straight up on ——

SCENE 11

Judith Loftus

*A kitchen with a dresser, on it are a pair of spectacles. Judith Loftus is
scurrying around, cursing, peering myopically about her. She's a touch
crazy: a fairy-tale figure*

Judith Where did I put the darn things? Where did I put my eye-glasses?
Where the devil are they? Some hobgoblin come in here and dance them
out the door! Husband say — keep 'em on a rope around yer neck. I'll put
a rope around *his* neck ... bringin' me here.

There is a knock at the door

Come in. *Come in!*

Huck enters, dressed as a girl

Hello — hello, my dear. Don't stand there useless ... come in and sit —
sit down!
Huck (*hesitantly shrill*) Why thank you!
Judith What's your name?
Huck Sarah Williams.
Judith Well, Sarah Williams — can you see them?
Huck See what?
Judith I got a pile o' mendin' — shirts and pants — and this old coat. I guess
I'll have to try without them.

Huck Without what?

Judith (*abruptly*) Whereabouts do you live?

Huck In Hookerville — seven mile below. I've walked — I've run from there ——

Judith I might've put my glasses in the dresser there. Will you look, child?

Huck finds the glasses and is about to proffer them, but Judith is off on a different tack

Tell th' honest truth — I hate the place. Nothin' but wind howlin' through, and rats. Rats as free as if they owned the place ... *there*! Look there!

She hurls a stone at a rat but — of course — misses by a mile

Blame creatures! Too damn fast for me. (*A beat*) You find them eye-glasses?

Huck (*a sudden decision*) No.

Judith Too bad. What was you sayin', child?

Huck It's my mother! She's sick — a snake bite. We don't have no remedy, an' I come to tell my Uncle Abner Moore an' see if he can help.

Judith Out on your own? It's not safe, child. A boy was murdered here five days ago.

Huck (*too eagerly*) Oh yes?

Judith You knew him did ya, child?

Huck Well ——

Judith A scoundrel by report — a scoundrel and a mischief-maker. Nothin' but a burden to his aunt ...

Huck No!

Judith What's that?

Huck (*covering up*) Who did the murder, then? This aunt?

Judith Some think the boy's father done it ... Will you be a honey and thread this needle for me? My eyes won't let me.

Huck pokes the needle at the thread without much success

Most everybody thought the father first. But then they changed right round and judged it was a runaway who done it — slave named Jim ...

Huck (*recklessly; in his boy's voice*) No! Not him — he's much too ——

Judith You knew him, too?

Huck (*caught out, very innocent; in his girl's voice*) No.

Judith Have you thread that needle, child?

Huck (*struggling*) There — no — there — no — there (*as a boy*) Ow! (*as a girl*) ow! — there, that's it.

Judith Why, thank you.

Huck Are they lookin' for the slave?

Judith There's a reward for him — one for old Finn, too. They'll get the slave real soon.

Huck (*alarmed*) Oh? Why?

Judith I noticed smoke on Jackson's Island yesterday. My neighbour tells me no-one lives there. I said to husband — well, might be worth the trouble to go down and give the place a hunt, so husband's goin' over later on tonight, him and two other men ...

Huck (*shaken*) Oh my, *oh my!*

Judith You ill, child? Why, you're shivering. Come here, child — Let me kiss you.

Huck grimaces and ducks away. Judith registers this

There now.

Huck I'm just fine ...

Judith (*after a beat*) Well, be a honey, take a stone and keep an eye out for those pesky rats. I can hardly see 'em.

Huck (*his confidence returning*) Sure thing, ma'am.

He picks up a stone and watches the skirting

Judith What did you say your name was, Honey?

Huck (*not thinking*) Mary — Mary Williams.

Judith Oh, Mary Williams, is it? I thought you said it was Sarah when you first come in.

Huck Sarah? Well — yes — I did. Sarah Mary Williams. My Uncle Abner always calls me Mary. It was his own poor mother's name ——

Suddenly, a rat scuttles by. Huck hurls the stone at it with real boyish brio

(*Boy's voice*) Bullseye! (*Girl's voice*) Bullseye!

Judith (*picking up the rat*) No, that was first rate. I'm very much obliged to you. I'm very much obliged.

She picks up the rat. It squeaks. She bludgeons it against the wall, then throws it in a bin

But, Honey, tell me — what's your real name?

Huck (*nervous*) What, mum?

Judith Now is it Bill, or Tom or Bob — what is it?

Huck Please to don't poke fun at a poor girl ——

Judith I ain't goin' to hurt you — and I ain't goin' to tell on you, nuther. You're a runaway prentice, that's all. It ain't anything. Tell me about it — your secret's safe with me.

Huck (*after a beat; bursting out*) It's no use tryin' to play it any longer. I'll make a clean breast, tell you everything. My father and mother is dead — and the law bound me and my brother to a mean old farmer in the country, thirty miles from here. He treated us bad — whip us and make us sleep in the yard — and so we took our chance, and I stole some of his daughter's clothes and we cleared out, and we bin three nights travellin' from there, and then last night my brother got bit by a snake and I's at my wit's end — and I believe you is my only hope.

Judith Hold on, child; I'll put you up a shot of remedy. There — get back to your little brother — bring him here when he can walk. We'll help you. But what's your real name, Honey?

Huck (*solemnly*) John Peters, mum.

Judith Well, John Peters, you do a girl tolerable poor — though you might fool some men, maybe. First — when you thread a needle, hold the needle still and poke the thread at it, and not the other way. Second — don't flinch so bad when someone makes to kiss you. Third, if you throw a thing, don't throw it like a cow-poke at a fairground. Miss first time.

Huck Yes ma'am.

Judith And can I have my glasses back? I need 'em for my sewin'. Though I can spot a story tall as yours at fifty paces.

A beat. They smile and shake hands

Huck runs

SCENE 12

The Raft

Smith Two hundred dollars for the drunkard Finn. Murderer of his child: infanticide, unnatural monster. Wanted dead or alive. Take no risks, good people: his depravity must threaten all. Finn will pay a dreadful price for murdering his sweet son, Huckleberry. Hunt him down. Arm yourselves well. He shall not, *must* not leave Jefferson County!

The island again

Huck — desperate, out of breath, half in/half out of his dress. Through the next speech, he hurls their possessions onto the raft — gun, blankets, bottles, fishing rod, whatever...

Huck Jim! I got the remedy, I got the remedy! Drink it down, drink it down.
You wait there while I load the raft — you take it easy. Three, four days,
you'll be just fine. I got to hurry. They're after us. There ain't a minute to
lose. I'll load the raft and then I'll help you down. You take it easy.

Jim A boat come by. Men lookin'. I tink some such ting. Mos' o' de truck
is on de raf' — I put it dere while you's away ——

Huck grabs the gun, then helps Jim hobble down to the raft

Boxes and bundles are piled at one side. Huck grabs a pole

Push her away, Huck — push her away!

Big river music. The raft spins out to mid-stream. Mist rises from under it.
Music to underscore

Huck Each morning — when the first streak o' day began to show, we tied
up at an island and hacked off branches to cover up the raft. At night we
headed on out to the main channel. We could run between seven and eight
hours, with a current that was makin' over four mile an hour. We catched
fish and talked and we took a swim now and then to keep off sleepiness.
It was kind of solemn, drifting down the big, still river — layin' on our
backs, lookin' up at the stars. The fifth night, we passed St Louis, and it was
like the whole world lit up.

Sound and lights give us some idea of this

Jim and Huck whoop with delight

SCENE 13

Kings and Frenchmen

Huck I reckon there ain't no king, there ain't no empr'r, there ain't nobody
on this earth more happy than me at this moment.

Jim Dat's f'sure, Huck, 'cos kings and empr'rs and such truck — dey only
in fairy stories.

Huck No. There is such men. I read about them at the Widow's.

Jim So. (*A beat*) How much do a king git?

Huck Why — they git a thousand dollars a month if they want it; they can
have just as much as they want; everything belongs to them.

Jim Ain't dat gay! En what dey got to do, Huck?

Huck They don't do nothin'! They just set around.

Jim Is dat so?

Huck They just set around. Except maybe when there's a war on. Other times, when things is dull, they fuss with the parlyment, and if everything don't go just so, he whacks their heads off. But mostly they hang round the harem.

Jim Dey ain't no kings *here* is dey, Huck?

Huck Well, I don't know.

Jim Dey can't git no situation. What dey gwyne to do?

Huck Maybe some of them gets in the navy, and some of them learns people how to talk French.

Jim (*after a moment*) Doan de French people talk de same way we does?

Huck No, Jim: you couldn't understand a word they said, not a single word.

Jim Well now — I be ding-busted! How do dat come?

Huck I don't know — but it's so. S'pose a man was to come to you and say "Polly-voo-Franzy" — what would you think?

Jim I wouldn't think nuffin': I'd take en bust him over de head!

Huck Shucks, it ain't *callin'* you anything. It's only saying — do you know how to talk French.

Jim Well, den, why couldn't he *say* it?

Huck Why, he *is* a-sayin' it. That's a Frenchman's way of saying it.

Jim Well, it's a blame ridiculous way, dey ain' no sense in it.

Huck Looky here, Jim: does a cat talk like we do?

Jim No, a cat don't.

Huck Well, does a cow?

Jim No, a cow don't nuther.

Huck Does a cat talk like a cow, or a cow talk like a cat?

Jim (*faintly irritated*) Only if you say so, Huck.

Huck It's nat'ral and right for 'em to talk diff'rent from each other, ain't it?

Jim Course.

Huck And ain't it nat'ral and right for a cat and a cow to talk diff'rent from *us*?

Jim It is.

Huck Well then, why ain't it nat'ral and right for a Frenchman to talk diff'rent from us? You answer me *that*!

Jim You may be right, Huck — I heard some such ting now I rec'lect. But answer me dis. Is a cat a man, Huck?

Huck No.

Jim Well den, dere ain't no sense in a cat talkin' like a man. Is a cow a man? — or is a cow a cat?

Huck No, she ain't either of them.

Jim Well den, she ain't got no business to talk like either one er the yuther of 'em. Is a Frenchman a man?

Huck Yes.

Jim Well den! Dad blame it, why doan he talk like a man? You answer me now.

SCENE 14

Slave Hunters

Smith and Pike enter

Smith (*suddenly*) You there!
Huck It's a skiff — two men in it. Git *down*, Jim!
Smith What you got there, boy?
Huck A piece of raft.
Pike Where you goin', boy?
Huck Way south, sir.
Smith Any men on board?
Huck Only one, sir.
Pike Well, there's a slave run off from way up river, boy. Maybe a murderer too. We're on his trail. Is your man black or white?

Silence. Huck is frightened

Is your man black or white?

Music. Suspense. "Real time" on hold

The Widow and Miss Watson materialize behind Huck

Widow What has poor Miss Watson ever done to you, that you could see her slave run off right under your eyes, and never say one single word?
Miss Watson What did I do to you, that you could treat me so?
Widow Why she only tried to teach you manners.
Miss Watson And to read!
Widow She tried to be good to you — every way she knew.
Pike Do you understand what I'm saying, boy? Is your man *black* or *white*?
Jim Don't tell 'em, Huck! Don't tell 'em! An' den we be jus' fine! An' when we reach de free state, why, den I save up money, never spen' a single cent till I's got enuf to buy my wife back, an' my chillen too ... an' if de master o' dem won' sell to ole Jim — why — I get an' ab'litionist to go en steal 'em!
Pike Do you speak the *language*, boy? *Tell me!* Is your man black or white?

A dark, sinister figure (the Preacher) emerges from the shadows

Preacher You know slave property is sacred, boy. To steal a horse or a cow is a low crime, but to help a hunted slave, or feed him, or shelter him, or hesitate to betray him to the slave catcher, is a *baser* crime ...

Pike *Is your man black or white?*

A noose drops from above

Preacher We hang ab'litionists. We don't waste no time. People come from miles around to watch them swing. They make a picnic of the day. And when the man is dead, the people buy the rope — ten cents an inch — to keep as a reminder of a job well done!

A long moment

Pike Answer me, boy! Is your man black or white?

We snap back to the present

Huck (*suddenly*) He's white!

The rope vanishes

The Preacher vanishes. The Widow and Miss Watson melt away

Music stops. Real time again

Smith Well, Mr Pike, I reckon we'll come and see for ourselves.
Huck (*panicky*) What?
Pike We're comin' over, boy. Buckle to, Mr Smith.
Huck (*improvising*) I wish you would!
Jim (*under cover*) *What!*
Smith What's that?
Huck I wish you would! — Because it's Pap that's here, and maybe you can help me tow the raft. He's sick!
Pike Oh the devil!
Smith We're in a hurry, boy — but I s'pose we've got to ...
Huck Pap'll be might obleeged to you. Everybody goes away when I want them to help me.
Smith That's infernal mean.
Pike Odd, too. Say, boy — what's the matter with your father?
Huck It's the — er — the well, it ain't anything much ...
Pike That's a lie! What *is* the matter with your pap? Answer up square now!
Huck I will, sir, honest — but don't leave us, please. It's the — the ——
Smith *Keep away, boy!* Confound it, I just expect the wind has blowed it to us. Your pap's got the smallpox, ain't he? That's the truth now, ain't it?
Pike Why didn't you come out and say so? Do you want to spread it all over?

Huck (*sobbing*) But I've told folk before — and they just gone 'n' left us.
Smith I feel mean to leave you, but it won't do to fool with smallpox — don't you see? Now — you keep back from us.

And they go

Jim peeps out from under the blankets

Jim Is dey out o' sight yit?
Huck They're gone.
Jim How you did fool 'em, Huck! Dat wuz de smartes' dodge!
Huck Tom Sawyer would be proud.
Jim You say you wuz happy as a king. I go far'n dat. Pooty soon I'll be a shoutin' for joy, 'en I'll say — it's all 'cos o' dat Huck; I's a free man, 'en I couldn't ever bin free if it hadn't ben for Huck. Huck done it. Jim won't ever forgit you, Huck; you's de bes' fren' Jim's ever had; en you's de only fren' Jim's got now!

Whoops, hugs, celebration

Huck On the fifth night after this ——

SCENE 15

Overboard

There is a sudden flash of lightning, and a deafening crack of thunder. Rain. Then — very close by — the sound of a steamboat's horn

Huck Jim! Look!
Jim A steamboat, Huck!
Huck Have they seen us?
Jim No! And dey's headed straight fur us!
Huck Look out, *look out!* Jump for it! Jump for it! Get clear, get clear ...

The drone of the oncoming boat and the crash of wood on wood overwhelms their voices. In the chaos, Jim and Huck are separated

The sound of the boat dies away, leaving Huck on land, soaked and desperate, running up and down the bank in the rain

Huck Jim! *Jim!* Where are you? Can you hear me? I'm on the bank — come here — *Jim!* Come on! If you can hear me — call out. *Jim!* (*Overcome*) We

should never've done this. I should've led you back to the Widder Douglas.
We could o' got along ... Jim! Jim! (*Very small*) Don't be drownded, Jim.

SCENE 16

The Grangerfords

Huck sinks to his knees. We see him in a tiny pool of light

*Then: the rain stops, warm late afternoon sun breaks through, and we hear
the sound of voices, singing a jaunty, oddball song. The Grangerfords sing
as they enter. Each carries a gun*

Grangerfords   We're the Grangerfords of the great mid-west,
We're generous, just and true!
Impeccably dressed in our Sunday best
We're Grangerfords through and through.

We're the Grangerfords of Arkansaw
Universally admired!
The Colonel and Ma and Buck and Bob,
Tom, Charlotte and Sophia!

And the ladies all display
Each feminine attribute:
They paint and play and sow and pray —
And hunt and fish and shoot!

Huck looks up, amazed, through this

*Now we can see the shutters and facade of a fine Southern mansion. Spanish
moss in abundance. Steps lead up to a door*

Huck (*calling*) Hello! Hello there!
Grangerfords   Our dogs are trained to fight,
With a nose for a pedigree —
They never growl or bark or bite
If you're aristocracee (like me!)
Southern aristocracee!
Huck Hello!

And this provokes a wild burst of barking from all round Huck

Colonel (*the fine old grandee*) I say — who's there? This is Grangerford property!

Bob (*wooden, handsome*) If you tell the truth — you've no need to be afraid.

Charlotte (*cheroot smoking*) But don't budge yit — we're all nigh perfect shots!

Tom (*Prince Charming*) We'll not hurt you. You have the word of the Grangerfords!

Sophia (*sweet, romantic*) He has an honest face …

Buck (*junior, a loose cannon*) Are you a Shepherdson? *I hope not.*

Ma (*charming old lady*) Speak up, boy, what's your name?

Huck George Jackson, ma'am.

Colonel What do you want?

Huck I don't want nothing, sir. I only want to go along by …

Colonel What are you prowling around for, hey?

Huck I warn't prowling around, sir. I'm lost.

Colonel What did you say your name was?

Huck George Jackson, sir.

Colonel Well, George Jackson — is there anybody with you?

Huck No, sir — nobody.

Colonel Do you know the Shepherdsons?

Huck No, sir — I never heard of them …

Colonel Well — that may be so — and it mayn't. How do you come to be lost, George Jackson?

Huck (*taking a deep breath*) Well, sir — Pap and me and all m'family was livin' on a little dried up dead hole of a farm at the bottom of Arkansaw, and my sister Mary-Ann run off and got married and we didn't know who to and she was never heard of no more, and Bill — he went to hunt them and he warn't heard of no more, and Joe and Mort died — Joe died in a fire, Mort died in a shoot-out, and then there weren't nobody but just me and Pap left — and he was just trimmed down to nothing on account of his troubles — so when he died, I took what was left — because the farm didn't belong to us — and started up the river, deck passage — and fell overboard. And that's how I come to be here.

Buck (*impressed*) What a story! Do we believe him?

Charlotte (*disappointed*) No threat.

Sophia (*compassionate*) He's an innocent: lost, abandoned.

Ma (*maternal*) The poor thing's as wet as he can be!

Bob (*ponderous*) I think we can say he isn't lying …

Tom (*generous*) He's no more a Shepherdson than you or me!

Much laughter at this

Colonel Very well! Give him a Grangerford welcome!

SCENE 17

One of the Family

The furniture is set during the opening lines of the scene

Ma There, George Jackson — I reckon you must be hungry. Corn beef, corn pone, butter milk, fried chicken and seed cake. Only a snack, I'm afraid.

Huck (*amazed*) Yes, ma'am.

Colonel My name is Grangerford. Colonel Grangerford. And this is my family. Now — that's Tom and Bob — they're my sons — and this is Buck, my youngest. This here's my wife — and over there, the finest looking girls in Arkansaw — my daughters Charlotte and Sophia.

Tom You're welcome, boy.

Bob Mighty glad to see you.

Buck Do you like riddles?

Colonel Look on this as your home.

Ma You can be another of our sons.

Charlotte There's good hunting around here.

Sophia And the boy that was lost, has been found.

Colonel *So!* What do you have to say for yourself, boy?

Huck (*wide-eyed*) Is this a palace?

Colonel It's where we live, boy.

Huck But where are the beds?

Colonel They're in the bedrooms, boy. Five in the south wing, six more in the north.

Tom A silver dollar for you, boy! (*Handing him the dollar*) You'll have no need to spend it while you're here.

A buzz of approval at his generosity

Bob I brought you down a clasp knife, George. (*He shows the knife*) It served my brother Frank until he died.

All God bless and keep him!

Colonel (*proudly*) He was a fine boy, and he died a brave death.

Bob (*giving Huck the knife*) I pray it brings you *his* good fortune, boy.

Colonel (*suddenly fierce*) Don't part from it, unless you leave it in a *Shepherdson!*

A tense moment

Tom A drink! A drink!

Immediate laughter, relaxation

Bob A glass of bitters!
Colonel Apple brandy for the boys …
Charlotte Whiskey for me!

Everyone gathers to arrange drinks

Sophia George Jackson. Here's a watch for you. It belonged to my brother Ben.
All God bless and keep him!
Huck Where is he?
Sophia Deep in the dark earth, George. We shall never hear his sweet chirrup more, alas.
All Alas!
Sophia (*suddenly*) I am in love, George. Only you know. Our secret, George … you'll be my special friend.
Tom ⎫
Bob ⎭ (*together*) Our duty to you, sir and madam!
Buck And here's to George Washington!
All George Washington!
Ma And the State of Arkansaw!
All The State of Arkansaw!
Colonel Strength to the Grangerfords——
All Confusion to the Shepherdsons!

All drink

Ma, the Colonel, Bob and Tom settle down to cards

Charlotte Can you shoot straight, boy?
Huck Five out of six at forty yards!
Charlotte The one you miss will be a Shepherdson. He won't miss you!
Huck (*nervous*) Why should he want to shoot me?
Charlotte You're one of us. Never fear. We'll practise in the yard tomorrow.
Buck And here's a gentleman's hat for you. And a question.
Huck Sure.
Buck Where was Moses when the candle went out?

Family attention: this is Buck's party piece

Huck (*uncomfortable*) Well, I don't know. I've not heard 'bout it before, no way.

Buck Well, guess!

Huck But how'm I goin' to guess, when I never heard tell about it before?

Buck But you can guess, can't you? It's just as easy.

Huck Which candle?

Buck Why, *any* candle.

Huck (*desperate*) I don't know where he was! Where was he?

Buck (*triumphant*) Why, he was in the dark! That's where he was!

Huck (*mystified*) Well — if you knowed where he was, what did you ask me for?

Buck Why, blame it, it's a riddle — don't you see?

Colonel (*changing the subject*) Before we go to bed — Sophia should entertain us!

Ma Why, yes, Sophia — read us one of your poems!

Tom That would be a treat!

Buck One of those nice short ones.

Bob Please, sister, please!

Colonel George hasn't heard you recite!

Charlotte Fire away, Sophie!

Sophia (*every inch the poetess*) George! This is an ode. My tribute to Stephen Dowling Bots: deceased.

> And did young Stephen sicken,
> And did young Stephen die?
> And did the sad hearts thicken,
> And did the mourners cry?
>
> No; such was not the fate of
> Young Stephen Dowling Bots,
> Though sad hearts round him thickened,
> 'Twas not from sickness shots
>
> Despised love struck not with woe
> That head of curly knots,
> Nor stomach troubles laid him low,
> Young Stephen Dowling Bots.
>
> Oh no. Then list with tearful eye
> Whilst I his fate to tell:
> His soul did from this cold world fly
> By falling down a well.
>
> They got him out and emptied him —
> Alas, it was too late.

His spirit was gone for to sport aloft
In the realms of the good and great.

Beat. Sniffs. Then loud, cheery applause

Buck (*to Huck*) Why — she can rattle off poetry like *nothing*! She don't even
have to stop to *think*! She ain't particular — she can write about anything
at all, just so it's sadful!
Colonel It's time for bed. Shall we pray.

The children kneel. Rather than praying, they sing, sotto voce:

Children   We're the Grangerfords of Arkansaw,
We're decent, honest and true;
We know what a bullet and a gun are for,
So we'll take good care of *you*!

And God saddles up in the heav'ns so blue,
And says "If this host of mine,
Could only shoot like the Grangerfords do,
We'd keep the devil in line (*just fine*)
We'd keep the devil in line!"

The Grangerfords are gone

SCENE 18

Harney Shepherdson

Music

Huck (*to the audience*) I liked all that family -- dead ones and all — and
thought I might never leave. Sometimes a stack o' people would come there
— mostly kin folks of the family — and stay five or six days — and have
such junketings round about, and on the river, and dances — and picnics
in the woods, day times — and balls at the house, nights.

*We see members of the family dancing under the stars. There is a starlit night
effect. The proceedings are interrupted by a sudden burst of rifle shots*

There was another clan of aristocracy around there: five or six families, all
by the name of Shepherdson.
Charlotte (*alert*) Two shots from an old musket — that's Buck; five from
a Winchester — not one of ours — rider on a horse ...

Ma Oh my Lord!

Colonel Prepare to saddle up! If one of those damned Shepherdsons has killed my boy — my youngest, my sweet child!

Charlotte No, that last shot was a musket — chances are the boy's alive.

Sophia (*emotional, improvising*)
>   The young boy stood before his foe,
>   Braver than Daniel, purer than the snow ...

Tom Bless us, Father. If we never see you again ...

This noble moment is spoilt by Buck's arrival

Huck Here he is! Here he is!

Buck enters — wildly out of breath

Buck I shep a Shotterson, I shap a Shetterson, I shottered a Stetterton!

All   } (*together*) {
>   Easy boy.
>   Calm down.
>   Take your time, Buck.
>   What happened?
>   Where have you been ...?

Buck The Snake Back Pass ... I'd laid down to watch for an old rabbit. I heard a horse ... I saw him coming ... I laid down — behind a bush — drew a line on him —*fired!* — only knocked his hat off — wish it'd been his *head*!

Colonel (*glowing with pride*) I don't like that shooting from behind a bush. Why didn't you step into the road, my boy?

Buck (*defensively*) The Shepherdsons don't, Father. They always take advantage.

Charlotte (*incredulously*) How could you *miss*! Were you above and to the side? How fast was he moving?

Tom I'm proud of you!

Ma We're *all* proud of you!

Buck He came after me ... I cut through the woods — ducked under Carrion Oak — down through the gully — the woods ain't thick there — so I looked over my shoulder, and twice he aimed at me, but then he rode away ...

Bob To get his hat?

Huck (*puzzled*) Who *was* this?

Sophia (*passionate*)
>   Who was the cold assassin?
>   Who rode the child down?
>   What murderer was cheated
>   Of infamy's dark crown!

Buck It was young Harney Shepherdson.

Sophia screams and faints

All *(simultaneously)* {
Sister!
Sophia!
What's the matter?
I think she's coming round!
Give her some air ...

Colonel Her heart is too great!

Ma *(to Buck)* She saw the danger you were in ...

Tom She knows how ruthless and how cruel he is!

Sophia *(coming round; oddly desperate)* It *was* only his *hat*? You did say it was only his hat!

Buck I fear so, sister.

Charlotte Don't blame him, Sophia — he's still young. Another year on the range, he'll blow his head clean off.

Sophia *(eagerly)* And he rode away — without a scratch?

Buck *(desolate)* Forgive me, forgive me — I did my best. I thought of Frank and Ben ...

Sophia *(laughing, almost madly)* I love you, Buck. Oh Buck — brave, young and brave. Ha ha!

They all look at her, puzzled. She takes a deep breath

Well — Harney Shepherdson will thank you.

After a second, much laughter at this

And I forgive you. For the shot you fired.

Buck I won't miss again.

Sophia You may not get another chance ...

The Grangerfords escort her off

Colonel *(to the audience)* Miss Sophia was awful pretty, but acted awful strange. I figured this was just a woman's way ...

SCENE 19

The Feud

Buck turns back

Huck Did you want to kill him, Buck?

Buck Well I bet I did!

Huck What did he do to you?

Buck Him? He never done nothing to me.

Huck Well what did you want to kill him for?

Buck Why nothing — only it's on account of the feud.

Huck What's a feud?

Buck Why, where was you raised? Don't you know what a feud is?

Huck Never heard of it before — tell me about it.

Buck Well — a feud is this way. A man has a quarrel with another man and kills him; then that other man's brother kills *him*; then the other brothers, on both sides, goes for one another; the the *cousins* chip in — and by and by everybody's killed off, and then there ain't no more feud. But it's kind of slow, and takes a long time …

SCENE 20

Clothes For The Poor

Suddenly, Sophia is with them

Sophia Now, George — you and me is goin' to the store at Paradise to get you a new set o' Sunday clothes …

Huck (*horrified*) No, *no*! I'm just fine the way I am!

Buck (*disgusted*) Why d'you want to comb him up and such kinds of foolishness?

Sophia And we'll take the old clothes to the mission for the poor folks. You'll help me carry them, won't you?

Buck Oh, Sophie …

Huck Well, I don't know …

Sophia You do like me, don't you, George Jackson?

Huck Indeed I do!

Sophia Buck here won't stir himself, and Father and the boys are always busy with the land …

Huck (*blushing*) Sure I'll help you with the old clothes, Miss Sophia …

Sophia And you will look so smart, George Jackson, in your new suit — that all the girls in town will fall in love with you …

Sophia returns with vanity bag, portmanteau, carpet bag …

Tom (*out of the window*) I hear you're givin' all your clothes to the poor folks, Sophie …

Sophia (*with immense bravado*) What the devil did you think I was doin', Tom? Runnin' off to marry Harney Shepherdson?

She laughs hysterically. And Tom laughs hysterically

Other Grangerfords appear, and the joke is passed on. Much laughter

SCENE 21

Paradise

Sophia drives away with Huck

Sound of carriage wheels. As they travel, she sings Stephen Foster's "If You've Only Got a Moustache". They arrive

Sophia George — you watch the trap. I have to meet someone at the hotel.
Huck What about the clothes for the poor folk?
Sophia Oh — we can bring those in another day ...

And she runs off

Huck is left, confused

Huck But — I thought these were the clothes for the ——

He walks up to the door of the hotel. It opens — and out steps ... Jim!

Jim *Huck!*
Huck *Jim!*
Jim Is dat *you,* Huck? En you ain't dead — you ain' drownded — you's back again?
Huck And you're alive, Jim — why, that's the best thing! I thought you wuz dead!
Jim It's too good for true, Honey, it's too good for true. Lemme look at you, chile, lemme feel o' you ... No! You ain't dead.
Huck Where you bin, Jim ... ? Why — you're dressed all smart and clean. What is this? You bin stealin'? How d'you git these things?
Jim When I got to de lan' — you wuz *gone.* I walks and walks, en den I finds a house.
Huck (*amazed*) And me!
Jim De biggest, most prop'rest house you ever saw. Like dem pictures o' Jericho in de good book ...
Huck (*faintly irritated*) My house was bigger than a palace. Eleven bedrooms, the parlor — size of a church!
Jim *My* house — twelve bedrooms — and de places for de horse 'n all, bigger'n de Widder's *whole house!*

Huck My house belongs to the biggest, most properest, finest folks in these parts ...

Jim No Huck — dat is impossible — dat is *my* house yo' describin' ...

Huck *Jim!* My house belongs to the *Grangerfords!*

Jim (*horrified*) Oh my Lord. Oh my sweet Lord! Oh *no*. Oh dat is de mos' darnes' ting dat ever wuz. Oh no oh no oh no ...

Huck Jim — *What is it?*

Jim Huck, Huck — we is de mos' deadly enemies. I's stayin' wid de *Shep'dsons!*

Huck The Shepherdsons?

Jim De Shep'dsons!

Huck But, but — they are the lowest, mos' terrible, damn foul folks in the whole *state*, Jim!

Jim *No!* — dat is yo folks, Huck — de *Grangerfords* — low down, cheatin', godless, thievin', no good stinkums!

Both *My people is the kindest, best, most lovin' gen'rous ...*

They stop — suddenly — and look at one another, abashed

Jim I bin de servant for dat Harney Shepherdson ——

Huck (*horrified*) *Harney?*

Jim I come wid him into town.

Huck He's here?

Jim In de hotel wid a young lady ...

SCENE 22

Elopement

At that moment, Harney and Sophia swing out of the hotel. He has a huge moustache

Music. He unloads her bags, and he and Jim take them offstage to their trap

Sophia Oh, George! What am I doin'? Where am I goin'? What wind carries me along? My heart beats faster than it ever did, my head is up there in the clouds. Without you, George, none o' this would have bin possible ...

Huck None o' what?

Jim (*in Huck's ear as he passes*) George?

Sophia Give this letter to my father, it explains *everything*. If they ask you — tell them I'm happy — happier than any person's ever been. Tell them — love clasped me to his bosom, and squeezed all the Grangerford out o' me. Tell them ——

Harney (*impatient*) *Sophia!* Your chariot awaits!
Sophia Oh Harney, Harney ...

A deep embrace. Huck and Jim are amazed

Goodbye, George, goodbye. God bless you!

And they exit

Sound of a carriage going. Silence

Jim Well, I be *ding-busted!* How'm I goin' to git home now? He took de trap!
Huck Oh Jim. There is goin' to be the mostest terrible row you ever did hear...
Jim Reckon dat won't be de *half* of it.
Huck Why — they kill each other for *nuthin'*. What are they goin' to do now
they *got* somethin'. What'll we do?
Jim Well — I bin a buyin' pots 'n pans 'n vittles, an' a-patchin' up de raf'
nights ...

Big river music

Huck The *raft*?
Jim Sure — our ole raf'.
Huck You mean to say our old raft warn't smashed all to flinders?
Jim No — she warn't. I found her and hid her. And now she's all loaded up
and ready to go.
Huck Oh Jim, Jim! You are the best and clev'rest an most lucky friend a
person ever had.
Jim But what we do now?
Huck Where's the raft?
Jim In de swamp — de place dey call Hog Bend —
Huck I got a stack o' things that we can take with us — a watch, a knife, a
gun, a book o' poems — a whole bag o' stuff. Money, too ...
Jim I sure hope dey gave you a book o' prayers.
Huck Why a book o' prayers?
Jim 'Cos we both goan to need dem ...
Huck Jim ... ?

SCENE 23

Armageddon

Jim indicates US

Behind them, the Grangerfords have arrived, armed to the teeth

Huck *(pale)* Why — Colonel Grangerford ... Charlotte ... Bob ... What are
   you doin' here?
Colonel *(lightning in his eyes)* George Jackson — where's my daughter?
Huck Your daughter?
Colonel Sophia. Where did she go?
Huck I — I think she went for a ride ...
Colonel Who was she with?
Huck *(brightly)* Why, *me*! I came to town with her. She said that she was
   goin' to buy me a new suit, an' ——
Colonel A suit. *A suit.* She bought herself a dress of shame, George Jackson.
   Who was she with?
Huck Some young fella.
Ma Better that she'd died when she was born. Better that she'd perished with
   the fever like little Emmeline. Better that I'd bin snuffed out by a
   Shepherdson before I ever had her!
Huck *(feebly)* She'll be back.

*But suddenly, shots ring out. The family form themselves into a group: brave,
eagerly heroic*

Tom An ambush!
Bob The Shepherdsons!
Colonel We're surrounded!
Charlotte I'll take a brace of them with me!
Tom Honour will be satisfied!
Bob Frank! Ben! We're comin' to join you!
Colonel Comin' on a path o' glory!
Jim Oh my sweet Lordy!
Huck We ain't got a chance! We ain't got a chance! Cowards! *Cowards*!

The group breaks up for a moment to clear up this misapprehension

Colonel *(indignant)* They ain't cowards, boy — not by a long sight!
Buck There ain't a coward amongst the Shepherdsons — not a one.
Bob And there ain't a coward amongst the Grangerfords either!
Tom No, sir — if a body's out huntin' for cowards, he don't want to fool away
   anytime amongst them Shepherdsons — becuz they don't breed any of that
   kind!

Another volley of shots

The family regroup. Jim jumps into a barrel, Huck hides amidst the Grangerfords. They start to sing and shoot. One by one they get shot — and die proudly, smiling as they go

> We're the Grangerfords of Arkansaw
> At last our chance is here —
> To die like heroes in days of yore,
> For reasons that ain't clear!
>
> For the Grangerfords of Arkansaw
> The moment of truth's arrived:
> A final chance to settle the score
> (Though none of us quite recall what for)
> And none of us may survive.
>
> We'll ride on up to heaven
> 'Cos the Shepherdsons only scored ...

And now it's only Buck left

Buck   Just five, and we got seven, Lord
                We'll get the big reward.

A final shot rings out and gets him. He looks cross

Damn you, Buck Shepherdson!

Just before he collapses, he shoots, and we hear another voice, away off, say "Damn you, Buck Grangerford."

A moment of silence. Huck crawls out from under the bodies

Huck (*horrified*) Oh no oh no oh no ... Colonel! Tom! Buck? Buck ...

But they are all dead. Jim pokes his head out

Jim Laws bless you, chile. I uz right down sho you's dead agin.
Huck (*in tears*) Jim, Jim ... they were my friends, they helped me!
Jim Dey ain't help you much like dis!
Huck I can't believe it, Jim. Jim — it's all my fault, I brought Miss Sophia here ...
Jim Huck, *Huck* — it's what dey wanted. I reck'n dey wuz aimin' for dis since dey come into de worl' ...

Huck But what are we goin' to do, Jim, where are we goin' to go?

Music

Jim (*grabbing him*) De *raf*, Honey! We ain't got no time t'lose. De *raf*! Let's clear outa dis place and not come back. De raf' is waitin' an' de big water an' another day! Le's get to de *raf* — we'z be comfy dere, and easy, and happy — and Huck — *we'll be free!*

The Big River theme reaches a crescendo

INTERVAL PROLOGUE

The Con Men

This Prologue has three phases: the first in the theatre foyer/bar; the second moving around the foyer/bar; the third just after the House Lights go down

PHASE 1

The Duke and the King set up their stalls in separate places in the foyer. The King should be near the bar with a temperance banner. He delivers a speech against drinking — maybe improvised, but along the following lines:

King Ladies, ladies — for seven nights now you have listened to me good. You have heard me warn you of the demon drink, an' how it turn a man into a version of the ragin' Beel-zee-bub. You've listened to m'tales of orphan chillen starvin' in the snow, of the rich and the splendid brought to beggary an' imposteration, of the honestest led into paths of jiggery-panky and hanky-pokery. I tell you, good people — and I thank you for the sweet ten cents that help to rescue drunkards from the deep, deep swamp of drunkardness — I tell you that Harold the King o' ole Englan' got the arrer in his eye — 'cos he was *drunk* — and couldn't see it coming for him; I tell you — that Goliath brought that temple crashin' down amongst the money-changers — becuz he was *drunk* — and did not see where he wuz goin'; I tell ya (and I swear to you this bottle only holds a good measure o' the good Lord's water from the good Lord's earth) that Socrates — the head teacher of ol' Oxford *drank hisself to death* on a gallon o' hemlock wine — an' — an' (would you ask the barman there for another draf' of water from the big brown bottle on the wall) an' that George Washington *hisself* was once a drunkard and a devilly demon before he heard the Lord's voice a-tellin' him to fly a kite and bring down lightnin' on a cherry tree to block the Redcoats at the Delaware ...

Meanwhile, the Duke is elsewhere with a chair, another of the Company sitting in it, and a small case of props

Duke (*dramatically*) What small town is this? What fate has led me here — I, who have touched the head of Franz Henry, the fifth king of all Austria,

and cured the Infanta of her whooping cough; She knew that I was a pupil
of the Great Mesmer and associate of his disciple Maxine de Pooceegar —
that Mesmer himself told me his great secrets with his dying breath. I,
Armand de Montalban, can release you from the grip of weasel melancholy,
unlock you from the chains of ravenous desire, draw from you superfluous
electricity that makes you wrathful, sad and tempted to rage at them as love
you. You, sir! You look as one whom the vile blows and buffets of
outrageous circumstance have brought to premature decrepitude. For fifty
cents I can infect you with a peace and sweetness of breath that any man
or dog would envy. For it is said by men of science that *ad hoc post
hominem virago est* — and if you will just permit me to tie you loosely to
this bowl of water — magnetized by Doctor Mesmer himself — I will
demonstrate with a passing of hands how all the apoplectic motions of the
body may be calmed, and the *gravitatio universalis* — the universal fluid
— restored to its smooth passage around your body. *There is no cure but
with belief!* Submit yourself, submit yourself — do not resist the feeling of
sleep that comes over you — calmness and sleep ... I pass my hands *over*
your head, *over* your eyes, I draw the stream of power out from the water,
through your body, and into my hands; out, through and into ... out,
through and away ... out, through and away ...

PHASE 2

*Four other members of the Company observe and then heckle these
performances. They drive both to a crisis point, two accusing the King of
being a secret drinker; two accusing the Duke of pick-pocketing as he passes
his hands over the patient. The Duke and King gather up their props and bags
and are pursued around the foyer/bar, appealing to the public for support.
They are finally chased backstage*

PHASE 3

The House Lights go down

The Duke and the King burst into the auditorium...

Duke ⎫ (*together*) Where ... Help ... They're after us, this way — Good
King ⎭   people, we didn't do no wrong — There's a way out at
                     the back ... No, no — it says *exit* over here ... Blamed
                     buildin' all steps 'n' seats — *Head for the river!* — *This
                     way*... Down this road ... Good Lard! — This is the
                     mos' amazin' offensive town I ever bin along 'v — Mad
                     men and Judases — Galoots and Lunkheads — Brayin'

mules and donkeys — They're after us — the dogs, the dogs ...
Have mercy ... (*Et cetera*)

And the townspeople come in pursuit

Sound of dogs barking; lanterns, torches, et cetera

Townspeople This way — they came this way —- good people, did you see
the swindlers? These men have cheated and robbed innocent men and
women — tar them! Roll them in feathers! Ride them on a rail! ... Stop
them before they do more harm — Teach them a lesson! (*Et cetera*)

*The chase goes up and down and round the auditorium. It should conclude
with the townspeople "outside"/in the auditorium — calling and shouting —
and the Duke and the King hurtling down to the stage*

Their torches pick out Huck and Jim on the raft

ACT II

SCENE 1

The Chase

Duke Boy! Save me! Rescue me! I am about to be robbed! A crowd of savage cut-throats is on my tail. Have mercy. Pull to the shore!

King I'm an ol' man, hardly able to move, unable to defend myself. Give me sanctooary. You boy are the gardjan cheroob-standin' t' deliver an innocent wayfarer ...

Townspeople (*from the auditorium*) Where are those villains? *Give yourselves up!* You can't escape! The sheriff an' half of Hard Times Arkansaw is after you!

The King and the Duke laugh embarrassedly/hysterically

Duke We're the victims of ——
King — a slight misunderstandin'
Duke We was only trying to help ——
King — some poor folks ——
Duke — an' old women ——
King — an' sick horses ——
Duke — an' cripples.
King We've got no friends.
Duke We're alone in the world.
King They were going to ride us on a rail!
Huck (*after a beat*) You two better climb aboard!
Jim Oh ma Lordy ...

And Jim and Huck extend hands/oars, grab bags, and help the Duke and the King on the raft

Music through this; also shouts from pursuing Lawmen ("Dang hang it! — the blamed dogs lost the scent ... We'll never find them now ... They's maybe swam out 'n the river ... Like as not they'll drown")

SCENE 2

Two Yarns

Huck and Jim pole the raft to mid river

The music stops

All four listen. Silence

Duke (*instantly boastful*) I've never thought quicker!
King A fine escape!
Duke I barely had to hurry ...
King Almos' too easy!
Duke (*to Huck*) You was lucky I came along, boy ...
King Another moment — they'd a bin on ya.
Duke But I gave them the slip!
King I said a raf' was th' only chance.
Duke I said the river would be our highway!
King I's of'en sailed out a' town like this.
Duke A raft is a stylish *modus transporti*!
King }
Duke } (*together, at each other*) But what got you into trouble?

A beat. Both relax a little. Maybe even rueful

King Well — I'd bin a-runnin' a little temperance revival thar 'bout a week, and was the pet of the women-folks, big and little, for I waz makin' it mighty warm for the liquor-boys, I *tell* you, an' takin' as much as five or six dollars a night — ten cents a head an' business a'growin' all the time — when somehow or another — a little report got round last night that I had a way of puttin' in my time with a private jug on the sly — Malicious falsehood! Suspicious spyin' tow-heads with their pryin' eyes on a man's medic'nal daily dose ... ! (*A beat*) That's my whole yarn. What's your'n?
Duke Mesmerism! I was practising the noble science and relievin' folks of their troubles and their melancholy and a tidy sum in fees — calling their true selves from deep inside a them, magnetizing their fluids and pulling them up 'n down 'n' round their bodies — and some darn snoop, some squeaking traitor made out that I'd slipped my hands inside the jackets of my patients and relieved them of their wallets! Well — I gave them the slip, but they were after me! The spies of the Volsces held me in chase 'n' I was forced to run!

A beat

Huck (*friendly*) So — where are you headin' for?
King (*neurotically*) *Stop asking us questions!*
Duke That's our darn business!
King What's it to you?
Duke (*horrified, pointing at Huck*) Another spy!
King His pap's prob'ly the sheriff!
Duke (*swooning*) Shall I never find peace ——
King We'd better scram ...
Duke — even in the seclusion of my private raft ...
Huck *Your* raft?
Duke And who are you anyways?
King *Yes!* Maybe *we* can do a little questionin'.
Duke I suspicion that this slave's a runaway!
King (*horrified*) A runaway? I'm calling back the sheriff.
Duke Now tell me straight, boy, before I call my friend the judge: *is he a runaway?*
Huck (*a brilliant reply*) For goodness sakes! *Would a runaway slave run South?*

A beat

Duke Very true ...
King South? Are we going south?
Jim De river flow dat way ...
King Is that so ... ?

The following lines are rapid cross-questioning

Duke Where'r you from, boy?
Huck Jefferson County, Missouri.
Duke And where's your family?
Huck (*sudden, persuasive tears*) A steamboat run over us. Jim and me come up, but Pa was drunk and Ike was only four, so they never come up no more. (*Pathetic*) An' ever since, me 'n' Jim bin travellin' alone ...
Jim (*just keeping up*) Folks all tink dat I's a runaway. How dey all comes out an' bothers us!
Huck (*very pathetic*) So now we travel nights. In secret. And alone ...

A beat

Duke That's very sad.

King (*sniffing*) My heart's in two bits.
Duke An orphan and a slave.
King I feel the tears coming.
Duke I am *deeply* affected. (*A beat*) *Very well.* You may travel with us! Welcome to my raft! I sleep on the straw tick, your bed's on deck. Old man! — you're welcome too. Now. What arrangements do you make for dinner?

SCENE 3

Wilks and Sherburn

The Lights shift suddenly to another part of the stage

Two men, armed, confront each other — Wilks and Sherburn. Wilks is an older man, a little unsteady on his feet; Sherburn is icy calm. Wilks' nieces, Susan and Mary-Jane cling to him

Wilks Turn and face me, Colonel Sherburn — turn and face me. We'll have this out at last.
Sherburn I'm tired of this. If you open your mouth about me once again, I'll draw against you, Wilks, and God have mercy on you then.
Wilks What do you know of mercy, Sherburn? Yes — we'll shoot this out, and you can add a new hide to the pile you've beaten from your slaves! There's not a man in town who don't appreciate your cruelty, though I'm the only one to speak against it ...
Mary-Jane Uncle Peter, I beg you to come in. How will this help?
Susan He will not listen. He has never listened.
Wilks We must draw a line and not go over that line. And step by step we shall move back from it.
Sherburn How I treat my slaves is my affair, Wilks.
Wilks (*to the crowd*) Will none of you speak up? Will none of you speak out? It's Peter Wilks — one that's helped you, worked with you, done business with you. But now you think I've lost my reason — don't you? Lost my senses ... "Oh, he's a fine fella — but he's crazy now — thinks that a gentleman like Colonel Sherburn here don't know what's best for women on his farm ——"
Mary-Jane No, Uncle Peter, no!
Wilks "— thinks that the Colonel here should mind his passions with a slave!"
Sherburn (*furious, icy*) *Very well!* I'll see you at the river's edge. Tonight at six o' clock! At six o' clock!
Wilks I'll meet you.

Sherburn If you fail me, sir, you can't travel so far but I will find you!

Sherburn strides away

Mary-Jane (*crying*) Uncle Peter!
Wilks There, there, don't cry. The time has come.
Susan You've got no chance.
Wilks (*excitedly*) But you see — I cannot lose.
Mary-Jane Follow him — say you are sorry — beg him to understand.
Susan Without you — we are alone.
Wilks No, no, no. My brothers will arrive. I have a letter from them only today. They docked at Long Island just two weeks ago. They'll take you back to England, to their home in Sheffield. I'm old and good for nothing now. Your uncles will look after you. It's for the best.

SCENE 4

The Duke and The King

Lights back to the raft

Some whiskey has been consumed

Duke (*to the King*) I reckon we might double team it together; what do you think?
King I ain't undisposed. What's your line, mainly?
Duke Jour printer by trade; do a little in patent medicines; mesmerism, teach singing and geography, sling a lecture ... theatre actor — if I like the part; tragedy, you know — a speciality. What's your lay?
King Oh — doctorin' an' layin' on o' hands. I k'n tell a fortune pretty good when I've got someone along to find the facts out for me. Preaching's my line, too. Any darn thing so it ain't work.

A beat

Duke (*suddenly*) Alas!
King What're you alas'ing about?
Duke To think I should have lived to have been leading such a life, and be degraded down into such company.

A sob

King Dern your skin, ain't the company good enough for you?

Duke Yes, yes — it *is* good enough for me; it's as good as I deserve. I don't blame you, gentlemen — far from it. I don't blame anybody. Let the cold world do its worst — take everything from me, loved ones, property, everything — but one thing I know, there's a grave somewhere for me. Someday I'll lie down in it, and my poor broken heart will be at rest!

King Drot your pore broken heart — what are you heavin' your pore broken heart at *us* fur ... ?

Duke I brought *myself* down.

King From whar?

Duke Ah, you would not believe me; the world never believes ... the secret of my birth.

Jim The secret o' your birth?

Huck What do you mean?

Duke Gentlemen — I will reveal it to you — for I feel I may have confidence in you. (*A beat*) By rights I am a *duke*!

Huck A duke!

Jim (*deeply impressed*) Oh my Lord!

Duke (*acknowledging the title*) Thank you.

King You can't *mean* it.

Duke Yes! My great grandfather — eldest son of the Duke of Bridgewater — fled to this country to breathe the pure air of freedom. The second son seized the title and estates, but before my great grandfather could dispute his claim, he died — leaving an infant son. I am the lineal descendant of that infant. I am the rightful Duke of Bridgewater, and here am I — forlorn, torn from my high estate, hunted of men, despised by the cold world, ragged, worn, heartbroken, and degraded to the companionship of felons on a raft!

Huck That's terrible!

Jim A dook! So — Huck, dere *is* such tings!

Huck I'm sorry for yer!

Jim Dat is de sadd'st story ever in de world!

The Duke cries a good deal

Huck Don't you be down-hearted.

Jim Don't take on so bad.

Huck Tom Sawyer'd know what to do ...

Jim Maybe de Pres'dent can do somethin'.

Huck He'll git that Robin Hood to help!

Duke No, *no* — of comfort no man speak.

Huck There must be *something* ...

Jim We'll do anythin'!

Huck Yes! Tell us — what can we do?

Duke (*sniffing*) Well …
Huck ⎱ (*together, eagerly*) Yes?
Jim ⎰
Duke Well … it would bring the wounded heart a little cheer if I might simply be *acknowledged*. That alone would do some good.
Huck ⎱ (*together*) How? Tell us how!
Jim ⎰
Duke Well …
Huck ⎱ (*together*) Yes?
Jim ⎰
Duke (*tentatively*) You might *bow* when you speak to me …
Huck ⎱ (*together*) Yessir!
Jim ⎰

They bow

Duke And address me as "Your Grace" — as in "Perhaps Your Grace would like a small glass of whiskey?" — or "My lord", as in "Of course, My lord, another ceegar" — and then, when we're informal you just call me Bridgewater, though not, *of course*, when you're waiting on me at dinner …
Huck ⎱ (*together*) *Of course!*
Jim ⎰
King (*a little put out*) Now jus' a momen ….
Duke Shall we practise?
King 'Fore y'all git goin' thar' …
Duke (*ignoring him*) Boy! What is on the menu tonight?
King (*impatient*) Listen!
Huck (*ignoring him*) I will consult the cook, Your Grace. Cook! What is on the menu for my lord tonight?
Jim Blamed if I know! Who dis Cook fella?
King (*very impatient*) Lookey here … !
Huck Catfish, Your Grace.
Duke I'll have it with a brandy sauce. And a bottle of Chateau Root Toot.
King *God darn it — will you listen!*
Duke (*peevish*) Not in front of the servants! (*To Huck and Jim*) You may go!

They have nowhere to go. But perhaps they get on with supper

King Lookee here, Bilgewater, I'm nation sorry for you, but you ain't the only person who's had troubles.
Duke No?
King No you ain't. You ain't the only person that's ben snaked down wrongfully out'n a high place.

Duke Alas!
King No, you ain't the only person that's got a secret of his birth.

And he starts to cry

Duke Hold! What do you mean?
King Bilgewater, kin I trus' you?
Duke To the bitter death! The secret of your being: speak!
King Bilgewater — I am the Dauphin.
Duke The what?
King Dauphin.
Huck
Jim } (*together*) The what?
King D—O—R—F—I—N.
Huck Dolphin?
Jim Orphan?
King (*crossly*) *Dauphin!* Yes, my friends, it is true — your eyes is lookin'
on the pore disappeared dauphin — Looy the Seventeen, son of Looy the
Sixteen and Marry Antonette.
Duke You! At your age! No! You mean you're the late Charlemagne — you
must be six or seven hundred years old at the very least!
King Trouble has done it, Bilgewater, trouble has done it; trouble has brung
these grey hairs and this premature balditude. Yes gentlemen, you see
before you — in blue jeans and misery — the wanderin', exiled, trampled
on and sufferin' rightful King of France.

And he cries and cries

SCENE 5

The King of France

Huck
Jim } (*together*) *The King of France*!
Huck How can we help?
Jim I's never bin so 'mazed!
Huck A duke *and* a king?
Jim Don't take on!
Huck Polly voo Franzy?
Jim You iz safe wid uz, Honey.
Huck Don't be mournful.
Duke (*sour*) So! The King of France ...
King It is cust'm'ry for folks like you to *kneel* when speakin' to the King.

Huck and Jim kneel

Duke *Quel surprise!*
King An' to 'dress me as "Your Majesty" — as in "Would Your Majesty care
for a helpin' o' this water-fowl before we shove it at the Dook?"
Duke I see …
Jim But we ain't got no waterfowl …
Huck (*hastily*) Surely will, Your Majesty!
King An' then — wait on me first at meals, an' don't sit down till I say so.
Huck ⎱ (*together*) Your Majesty!
Jim ⎰
King An' wash my socks an' linen an' such like.
Huck ⎱ (*together*) Yessir!
Jim ⎰
King Well, thank you! That'll do just dandy.

A beat

Duke Well. Quite a coincidence ——
King Bilgewater?
Duke — the King of France, showing up in Arkansaw.
King Yup.
Duke Under such depressing circumstances.
King Sure.
Duke And in so delapidated a condition.
King An' then think of it — runnin' into a Dook!
Duke (*measured*) I must remind you that the aristocracy of old England ain't
ever bin too partial to the Kings of France.
King What d'you mean?
Duke At Crécy and Agincourt, at Harfleur and Waterloo — the Dukes of old
England have taken stupid ol' Kings of France, and beat their hides until
they *squealed*!
King Now — easy does it Bilgewater!
Duke (*relentlessly*) Shall another glorious victory be proclaimed? Shall the
French monarch suffer a watery defeat at Hard Times, Arkansaw? Shall
gentlemen in England now abed think themselves cursed they didn't see
the Duke of *Bridgewater* throw the *Dorphin of France* in the *Mississippi
River*!

A beat

King Servants! Shift! (*Confidentially to the Duke*) Like as not, we got to be
together a blamed long time on this h'yer raft, Bilgewater, an' so what's

the use of your bein' sour? It'll only make things uncomfortable. It ain't my
fault I warn't born a duke, it ain't your fault you warn't born a king — so
what's the use to worry? Make the best of things, that's my motto. Come,
give us your hand, Duke, and let's all be friends!

A beat. Then — rapprochement! Smiles, bonhomie

Duke Well, Royalty! It's a privilege to know you. Tell me — have you ever
trod the boards?
King No indeed, I have not, Bilgewater.
Duke You shall then, before you're three days older, Fallen Grandeur. The
first good town we come to — we'll hire a hall — and put on a show. Our
servants can help.
Huck ⎫
Jim ⎭ *(together; promptly)* Your Grace!

Scene 6

The Letter

*Lights up on a night-time scene. Miss Watson — pale and faint and shrunken
— sitting by a window*

Tom Sawyer enters and the Widow behind him

Tom *(addressing the audience)* In the streets of St Petersburg — Huckleberry
Finn was not forgotten. No more was Jim. At night if you was passin' by
the Widow Douglas' house, you'd hear a keenin' and a moanin' fit to break
a person's heart. Miss Watson took Huck's death real bad.
Widow *(coming forward)* Esther? Esther, my dear — what are you starin'
at?
Miss Watson The river. The bend in the river. I'm waitin'.
Widow *(to Tom)* All day — she stands here all day an' half the night, waitin'
and watchin'.
Miss Watson *(feebly)* Who's there? Who is that?

A beat

Tom Only me, Miss Watson.
Widow Here's Tom Sawyer come to see you, Esther. Say hello to him.

Miss Watson peers at Tom. A look of astonishment comes over her face

Miss Watson You've come … you've come.

Widow (*nervously*) Esther — it's only Tom.

Miss Watson (*straining, but unable to get out of her chair*) I've waited for you — oh so long — I've waited for you. Oh my heart. You're here again. My boy, my Huckleberry. You've forgiven me. Look, Martha, look, he's back — he's here! Give him a bite o' food, he must be famished. He likes an apple, a good red apple, give him a piece of apple …

Widow No, *no*. It's Tom Sawyer. Huckleberry's friend — Tom Sawyer.

Miss Watson (*not hearing*) I should've gone and fetched you — fetched you back. I left you there, I left you.

Widow Oh, Esther.

Miss Watson Now Huckleberry. You must do a thing for me — a simple thing. Say that you will — oh say you will.

Tom (*intrigued*) Of course, Miss Watson. Anything.

Miss Watson You must find Jim. Say to him I never needed those eight hundred dollars. I never needed them. I needed him and now I've lost him. You find him, Huckleberry. Give him this letter. Promise me you'll give it to him.

Tom You have my solemn word.

Miss Watson Guard the letter with your life. And swear to me that you won't open it.

She reaches out suddenly, grasps his hand and pulls him towards her

Swear on this Bible here that you will find him, Huckleberry, and give him this.

Tom I swear.

SCENE 7

The Rehearsal

It is now late at night on the raft. Dinner is over and much whiskey has been drunk. Perhaps we catch the end of a song

Duke Well, Rex — we'll want to make this a first-class show, you know, so I guess we'll add a little more to it. We want something to answer Encores with, anyway.

King What's Onkores, Bilgy?

Duke It's the *French*, Monsieur le Roi, for what we do when we're a *triumph* and all the Jakes and Lunkheads who have never seen the like of us — beg for another morsel from our table! Oh! I've got it! I could do Hamlet's soliloquy!

King His which?
Duke Hamlet's soliloquy — you know — the most celebrated thing in
Shakespeare. Ah! It's sublime, sublime! Always fetches the house. I
haven't got it in the book — but I reckon I can piece it out from memory ...

A quantity of preparation here. He pulls faces, moans, sighs, cries, mutters
and gargles. Then "rips and raves and grits his teeth" and "howls and swells
his chest"

>To be or not to be; that is the bare bodkin
>That makes calamity of so long life;
>For who would fardels bear,
>Till Burnam Forrest come to Dunsinane
>But that the fear of something after death
>Murders the innocent sleep
>Great nature's second course,
>And makes us rather sling the arrows
>Of outrageous fortune
>Than fly to others that we know not of.
>There's the respect must give us pause —
>Pause and resolve itself into a dew,
>For who would bear the whips and scorns of time,
>The oppressor's love, the proud man's insolence,
>The clown's delay, the jibes the gambols and the songs
>And the quietus which his pangs might take
>In the dead waste and middle of the night
>When churchyards yawn in customary suits
>Of solemn black,
>But that the undiscovered country
>Seems to me a sterile promontory
>And *thus* the native hue of resolution
>Like the poor cat i' th' adage
>Is sicklied over with the dogs of war
>And all the clouds that lowered upon our house
>With this regard droppeth their rain from heaven
>And lose the name of action.
>'Tis a constellation devoutly to be wished.
>But soft you, the fair Ophelia!
>Ope not thy ponderous and marbled jaws
>But get thee to a nunnery — go!

And then a flourish. Huck and Jim applaud wildly

It's the Folio version, of course. Now — the balcony scene — how does
that strike you?

King (*very drunk*) I'm in, up to the hub, for anything that will pay, Bilgewater
— but I hain't ever seen much of play-act'n. I was too small when Pap used
to have 'em at the palace. Can you larn me?

Duke Easy!

King All right. Tell us about it.

Duke Romeo — an Italian prince — son to the Montagues — young,
handsome, irresistible to women. That's me. Juliet — young, innocent,
pretty as a picture, daughter to the Capulets. That's you.

King But ——

Duke Good. That's settled then. Well — I'm for turning in. Come, King of
Kings, I think I feel the arms of Morpheus about me.

King (*now completely legless*) 'as *right*, Bilgy — more for us — more for
me, more for you ... in *arms, and more for us*!

*They stagger to the back of the raft and collapse. Singing, snores — then
silence*

SCENE 8

The Duel

A patch of ground by the river's edge. Near sunset

Wilks It's time.

Mary-Jane God bless you.

Wilks This is *His* land, Mary-Jane, (*gesturing at Sherburn*) not his. It's never
looked so fine. The river and the cotton woods, the sky reddening up; the
breeze cool and fresh and sweet to smell. I'm glad to die here.

Sherburn Begin!

Wilks (*to Mary-Jane*) Remember me to my brothers. I'm sorry that I
couldn't stay to see them. Harvey and William will understand. (*A beat*)
Goodbye.

He draws away from the girls

I'm ready for you, Sherburn.

*A long beat, then Wilks lifts his gun and fires. Sherburn; unscathed, fires his
gun. Wilks falls. Mary-Jane screams and runs to the body*

SCENE 9

Roll-up, Roll-up

Huck appears in a spotlight — calling to the population of the town

Huck Ladies and gentlemen! Shakespearian revival! Wonderful attraction! For one night only! The world renowned tragedians, David Garrick the Younger of Drury Lane, London, *and* Edmund Kean the Elder, of the Royal Haymarket Theatre, Whitechapel, Pudding Lane, Piccadilly, London — and the Royal continental theatres, in their sublime Shakespearian spectacle entitled "The Balcony Scene in *Romeo and Juliet!*" Romeo to be played by Mister Garrick, Juliet by Mister Kean, assisted by ... (*nervously, looking around*) ... assisted by the whole strength of the company! New costumes, new scenery, new appointments. Also: the thrilling, masterly and blood-curdling broad sword conflict in *Richard the Third* with Mister Garrick as Richard the Hunchback King and Mister Kean as his valliant foe, Richard. For one night only!

SCENE 10

'Lizabeth

The hall hired by the Duke for their big performance. Huck and Jim rehearsing

Jim So — git you down t' Friar Lawrence cell!
Huck (*to the audience*) The night before we played that balcony scene, Jim was tryin' to git his role by heart ...
Jim   So — git you down t' Friar Lawrence cell!
                                    I'll make you a husban' an' you a wife!
                                    Den smile de heav'ns upon dis holy act
                                    Dat after-hours wid sorrer chid uz not ...

Dis ain't like any person I's ever heard talk! Why he got to say d'ting so darn com'licatory?
Huck It's how they talk in *Italy*!
Jim Darn them! I thot it was some such ting. What do it mean?
Huck Well — he hopes it's all going to turn out dandy.
Jim What?
Huck Why — Romeo marryin' Juliet — and all that.
Jim And do it?
Huck *I* don't know ...

Jim It ain't likely. (*Beat*) I married Dorothy — and five year on, we was split apart. Miss Watson kep' me — but she sole Dorothy an' little 'Lizabeth an' little Johnny.

Huck I know.

Jim Better dat I never married her. Better dat I never seen her.

Huck No!

Jim Why?

Huck (*confused*) Sure I don't know why, Jim.

Jim It makes like I were *never* hers, an' she were never really mine. An' all I kin r'member is de times I treat dem bad. (*A beat*) Little 'Lizbeth was fo' year ole 'en she tuck de skyarlet fever — but she got well. 'En one day I says to her "Shet de do" — but she never done it, jis stood thah kiner smilin' up at me. It make me mad. I says agin "Doan you hear me? Shet de do'!" She just stood de same way, kiner smilin' up, an' so I fetch her a slap side de head dat sent her a'sprawlin' — but den — 'long come de wind 'en slam de do behine de chile — *Ker — Blam!* — 'en ma lan' — de chile never move. My breff mos' hop outer me. *She never budge!* Oh Huck I bust out a-cryin'. She was plumb deef en dumb, Huck, plumb deef en dumb — 'en I'd ben a-treatin' her so ... Does are de tings I r'member Huck. An' losin' dem. So 'dis Romeo — he done better not to trus' de heav'ns over much when it come to *marryin'*.

SCENE 11

Trader Pike

Another area. A flickering torch

Sherburn and Pike

Sherburn The descriptions fit.

Pike I was in Hard Times the day before they left. One old and bald — the other younger — with the cheek o' the divil.

Sherburn But who are their associates?

Pike A boy ...

Sherburn A boy and *one other*.

Pike Tall — hidden away mostly, or hooded like an old eagle.

Sherburn It's a runaway, Pike — believe me, I can smell a runaway in the next state. But what if it should be *our* runaway ... Missouri Jim.

Pike The biggest, strongest slave I ever seen. A giant. The deal was almost done and then he ran.

Sherburn If it were him! Think of that, Pike — think of that!

SCENE 12

The Balcony Scene

*The Lights change to suggest an old-fashioned playhouse. Footlights and so
on. The hecklers are out in the audience*

The Duke enters — very romantic

Duke   "But soft what light through yonder window breaks?
                        It is the east and Juliet is the sun!"

*The King turns round on a precarious balcony. He's dressed in a nightgown
and ruffled night-cap. No attempt has been made to disguise his beard*

Heckler 1 It's a grizzly bear!
Heckler 2 Why — she's mighty like your wife, Brer Hotchkiss!
Heckler 1 But younger!
Heckler 2 And pootier!

Raucous laughter

King   "Oh Romeo, Romeo ..."
Duke (*through clenched teeth*) Not yet! Not yet! Your cue is "touch that
    cheek".
King What?
Duke (*loudly*) Touch that cheek!
King   "Oh Romeo, Romeo ..."
Duke No! *NO! Amateur!* — I have more to say.
Heckler 1 Git on with it!
Heckler 2 Let the bearded woman *speak!*
Duke   "It is my lady, oh it is my love;
                        Oh that she knew she were!"
King (*hopefully*)   "O Romeo ..."
Duke (*emphatically*) "She speaks *yet she says nothing. What of that?*
                        See how she leans her cheek upon her hand
                        O that I were a glove upon that hand
                        That I might touch that cheek.
                        That I might touch that cheek!"
Huck (*helpfully*) Oh Romeo, Romeo ...
King (*wrathfully*) *I know!*
                        "*Romeo, Romeo,* wherefore art thou *Romeo!*
                        Deny thy father and refuse thy name
                        And I'll no longer be a Capoolet."

Duke   "Call me but love and I'll be new baptised
                Henceforth I never will be Romeo."
King   "Art thou not Romeo an' a Montagoo?"
Duke   "Neither fair maid ——
Heckler 1   Make up yer darn mind!
Duke   — if either thee dislike."
King   "This place is death
                If any of my kinsmen find thee here."
Duke   "I have night's cloak to hide me from their eyes
                And but thou love me, let them find me here."

King (*he hasn't quite learnt this speech*) The mask of night is on my cheek...
Or else a maiden blush would make it red ... Dost thou love me ? — Ay,
yes, say — and then, ah then, I'll say yes too — but don't swear — no,
don't— or Jove will *laugh* — laugh at your swearing ... and if you think
this is all a litt'l hasty — then I'll back off and say nay — *nay* ...

Heckler 1   Is she a horse?
King *Nay!*
Heckler 2   She's an old mule!
King   If thou wilt — *woo.*
Heckler 1   It's an owl!
King   "I love you and it's true,
                true — a true love's passionate true love ... it's true ..."

He peters out. The Duke is very still

(*Bashfully*) Summat like that?
Duke (*very calm*) More or less. Shall we proceed? (*A beat*)
                "Lady! — by yonder blessed moon I vow —"
King   "No, no — do not swear ... I have no joy in this tonight!"
Heckler 1   We're with you, gal!
Duke   "Oh wilt thou leave me so unsatisfied?"
Heckler 1   Give her a kiss!
Heckler 2   We'll hold the back legs!
King (*very daintily*) "No no — good night! Parting is such sweet sorrow
                That I shall say goodnight till it be morrow."
Duke   "But stay, but stay!
                I have a Friar brought ..."
Heckler   Chicken for me!
Duke   "Who can in holy wedlock join our hands
                Let him come forward and perform the rite,
                And all my fortunes at thy foot I'll lay
                And follow thee sweet chuck through all the world."
King   "Now down I come from this my balcony
                To see a Friar, if Friar I can see!"

Awkward and noisy descent from balcony

Duke Friar! Come forth!

A much hooded Jim edges on to the stage

Jim (*rather fine*) "So git you down to Friar Lawrence cell
I'll make you a husban' an' you a wife
Den smile de heav'ns 'pon dis holy act
Dat after hours wid sorrer chid us not ..."

A long moment

During this speech Sherburn and Pike — heavily armed — have appeared in front of the stage. At last nobody can ignore them

Sherburn I don't trust this Friar. I want to see his face.
Duke (*coming forward; charming*) But this is his costume, sir. A friar of the period would certainly have worn a full cowl and ——
Sherburn I'm not interested in your cowls and costumes. Pike!

And Pike moves on to the stage towards Jim. Jim backs off. Tension. Pike reaches up and snatches the hood back. Gasps from the audience

So! Missouri Jim. At last — I've got you, boy.
Pike You give me the slip once before — you won't do it agin.
Sherburn I'll pay your old mistress the eight hundred dollars I promised her — and then you're mine, boy. To do with as I like.
Pike An' you others — well — your necks'll need a bit o' stretchin' I reck'n. Helpin' a runaway. That's awful bad.

Pike has come face to face with the Duke

Duke (*very still*) The love I bear thee can afford no better term than this; thou art a villain.
Sherburn Your play-acting is over boy — you come along with us.
Duke This shall not excuse the injuries that thou hast done me, therefore turn and draw!
Pike What the sweet heck d'you think you're doin'?
Duke Tybalt, you ratcatcher, will you walk?

And all hell breaks loose. A big fight. Sherburn fires his gun

Lights out

Scene 13

A Payment

Lights up on a tableau

Jim under arrest

Sherburn You're mine! Missouri Jim. But Pike — I want this thing done right. Get back to Petersburg. Renew my offer. Here: eight hundred dollars for Miss Watson. Don't be distracted on the journey.
Pike I wouldn't compromise your profit.
Sherburn Don't let me down this time. You know I don't forgive easy.
Pike (*nervous*) I've got the money. I'll be in Petersburg by Friday.
Sherburn And here again the next evening. I want that bill of sale, Pike. I want it very badly.
Pike I'm sure you do.
Sherburn There's something soft and rotten about you, Pike. Don't let me think I've finished with you. Don't let me think that, Pike.

Scene 14

Caught!

Outside the town. Huck — out of breath, half-in/half-out of costume — desperate. The Duke and the King are panting, agitated

Huck Jim, Jim! Where is he? Jim!
King Keep the noise down, boy — they'll find us!
Duke We lost them, I think we lost them.
Huck I'm going back.
King Is you *mad*?
Duke They think he's a runaway. You helped him. If they catch you —
King — yer dead.
Huck But he's my *friend* — the only friend I have in the world!
King He's a slave, boy. Don't be a darn fool!
Duke (*tersely*) They got him. I saw it happen. They'll beat him, hang him. You won't see Jim again.
King He ain't only but a slave!
Duke You're coming along with us, Huckleberry. You squeal — we're all dead.
Huck But sir ...
Duke (*nastily*) Shut it! Shut it now, kid — or you won't make it to the river.

King (*nervously*) Bilgewater! Have y' got the takings?

Duke Safe and sound, Majesty. Now Huckleberry — tomorrow, bright and early, you buy us new clothes — I'll show you where. King, look at this.

King What's this?

Duke A local news sheet.

King Oh — a review?

Duke No, no! Our friend Sherburn killed a man not twenty miles from here — an abolitionist called Wilks. Now look — Wilks' brothers are expected any day from England to claim their just inheritance ...

King (*sour*) Well, I'm mighty pleased for them, I'm sure ...

Duke For *us*, majesty, for *us*. How's your English accent?

King (*light dawning*) Oh ...

Huck But Jim ...

Duke *Don't spoil it, boy.* Ancestral longings are upon me. Come, Royalty — I am fortune's steward. Come boy, you shall partake of lucky joys and golden times. What's done is done! The future calls!

And they disappear into the darkness

Huck turns to the audience. In the background, we see Jim chained in Sherburn's dungeon. He is humming the lullaby that opened the show

Huck I could see Jim before me — in the day and in the night time, sometimes moonlight, sometimes storms — and we a-floating along, talking and singing and laughing. I'd see him standing my watch on top of his'n, 'stead of calling me, so I could go on sleeping, and see how he would always call me honey, and pet me, and do everything he could think of for me, and how good he always was — and at last — how he said I was the best friend old Jim ever had in the world and the *only* one he's got now. An' I thought of the preacher and the rope and Miss Watson sayin' I'd go off to hell. An' I thought "All right then, I'll *go* to hell — I'll follow those two liars and go to work and steal Jim out of slavery again." (*A beat*) Becuz I saw he were the best friend *Huck'd* ever had ... And just that time — I thought I'd never find another.

SCENE 15

A Chance Meeting

A dark street in St Petersburg. Tom Sawyer hurries home. The sinister figure of Pike stops him

Pike You boy!

Tom You startled me!

Pike I don't get no answer at this door.

Tom That's because the owner's gone away.

Pike Away?

Tom The Widow Douglas — left for Boston and her cousin there.

Pike So where might the other woman stay?

Tom Miss Watson? Why, she's staying out of doors just now.

Pike (*frightened*) What do you mean?

Tom She has a comfortable lodging ... in the cemetery. She won't be coming back. She likes it there.

Pike No — *no!*

Tom I didn't put her there.

Pike (*agitated, to himself*) What's to be done, what's to be done? It's all up with me. I had to see her. I had to get the bill of sale. I had to take it back. He'll kill me — don't you see — he said he would ——

A beat

Tom P'raps I can help you, sir.

Pike P'raps you *can't*.

Tom My name's Tom S — Watson.

Pike So?

Tom (*improvising*) Tom Watson. I'm her nearest living relative.

Pike Good — good!

Tom (*airily*) Her whole estate was left to me: house, beds, gold, land ...

Pike Slaves?

Tom (*startled*) Miss Watson didn't have no slaves ——

Pike Missouri Jim.

Tom He ran away.

Pike I caught him. I caught him — and I badly need to buy him ...

Tom Where is he?

Pike That's my business.

Tom Well, Mister —— ?

Pike Pike.

Tom Well, Mister Pike: why don't we step inside and talk. I might be travelling in your direction.

Scene 16

Harvey and William

Mary-Jane is reciting from the scriptures. The scene is the Wilks' parlour. The coffin containing Peter Wilks' body stands on trestles

There is a sudden commotion from outside

Susan bursts in

Susan They've landed, Mary-Jane, they've landed — and they're coming up from the jetty, the two of them. I never thought ... and such a distance...
Mary-Jane Calm yourself, Susan. Who is it that's landed?
Susan Why — our uncles, Mary-Jane: Harvey and William — fresh off the six o'clock boat. Oh, Mary-Jane — what shall we do?
Mary-Jane Compose yourself, Susan, straighten your dress, and don't bully them when they arrive.
Susan England — and Sheffield! Think of it. Will we be welcome though? After Charlottesville ... Have they forgiven us?
Mary-Jane Be quiet. And remember, Susan, to be patient with your Uncle William. Smile gently at the poor creature — and address yourself to your Uncle Harvey.

The sound of a crowd outside, talking excitedly

Oh my goodness — there they are. This moment ... so long awaited. I mustn't weep. Susan, give me your hand.

Loud knocking at the door, which opens to reveal — the Duke and the King! They are both dressed smart and formal — the King as a preacher. Huck is right behind with the bags

King (*in a terrible English accent*) Is this where my dear brother Peter lives?
Mary-Jane Oh sir — it's where he lived until two days ago.
King Why no! You cannot mean ...
Susan He's dead, he's dead. Murdered!
King No — no! (*Apparently overcome with emotion, turning to the Duke*) Alas, alas! Our poor brother — gone, and we never got to see him; oh, it's too too hard.

The Duke bursts into tears

Duke (*in a stage whisper to the King*) You see, this is the one place Sherburn can never look for us!
Mary-Jane How wonderful that he can understand you.
Susan A miracle!
Bell Hallelujah!
Mary-Jane And though he heard not the hoot of the owl nor the crack of the thunder — he was not neglected of God.

King Oh, he'll make himself understood!
Duke (*trying to say "good-morning"*) Goo —
Susan But imagine.
Duke Goo ——
King He's *never* at a loss ——
Susan — able to let you know his thoughts ——
King — difficult to hold him back most days ——
Susan — when poor Uncle William ——
King I'll hand you over to him right now!
Duke Goo ——
Susan When Uncle William has been deaf and dumb since birth.

A long moment while the Duke digests the implications of this

Duke Goo goo goo.
King (*delighted to be in the driving seat*) You must be Mary-Jane.
Mary-Jane Yes!
King And this — dear Susan.
Susan Oh, yes — I am!
King I am your Uncle Harvey and this — this is poor dear William.
  (*Gesturing at Huck*) That is Adolphus — he's my valet.

More kisses

Huck (*turning to the audience*) How did they manage this?
King Never to see him again — the dearest and the kindest, the sweetest and
  the gentlest; the victim of a murder! (*Addressing the audience*) Friends,
  good friends …
Huck By and by the King slobbers out a speech, all full of tears and
  flapdoodle ——
King Good friends of the deceased …
Huck *It was just sickening! All soul butter and hogwash! I never see anything
  so disgusting!*
All Hallelujah!
King (*fishing*) Our dear brother Peter wrote to us so often 'bout you folks —
  about dear — (*hazards a guess*) — John …
Abner Why yes, John Hightower over there — the miller. And here is Judge
  Bell —
Bell You're welcome, Harvey Wilks.
King You're welcome too. It's an honour.
Abner And I'm Abner Shackleford.
King It is a great honour.
Abner No, no — it's a greater honour for me.

Bell No — it's a greater honour for me.
Abner And here's Doc Robinson.
King No — it's a greater honour for him.

The Duke throws his hat at him

Doctor You say that Peter wrote to you. How often did he write?
King Every month! Long, loving letters — letters to tear the heart out of a body.
Doctor That's strange — he told me that he hadn't heard from you in years.
King (*without missing a beat*) What! Did my letters never arrive? — Did he never hear from me? Or receive the sweet paintings that my brother sent?

More gesticulation at the Duke

Bell Mary-Jane — tell them of your Uncle's will.
Mary-Jane Why yes, of course.
King A will? But why should that concern us?
Doctor You are the dead man's loving brothers …
King He knew we crave no earthly riches — riches profit not in the day of wrath.
Abner (*with fervour*) If riches increase — set not your heart on them.
Susan God has spoken once; twice have I heard this.
King Twice? Thrice! — Riches? Riches? — What are riches? … Riches … (*A beat*) Well. Riches. Mmm.
Mary-Jane (*reading*) I charge my brothers Harvey and William with the welfare and prosperity of my nieces Mary-Jane and Susan—
King (*not entirely good news*) Oh.
Mary-Jane — the just performance of which obligation renders these two brothers my principal beneficiaries.
King (*immediate change of mood*) Of course! At once! My dear, dear girls. You'll be to us as daughters, loved ones, precious daughters of Jerusalem, precious loved ones of Judah …
Doctor (*laconic*) Nieces.
Susan Tell your brother, Uncle Harvey.
King (*carried away*) I think we all heard the good news! What d'ya say, William …
Duke (*emphatically*) Goo goo goo *goo*!
King (*turning on a sixpence*) Even after all these years, I still forget.
Mary-Jane I bequeath to Harvey and William Wilks all my property, the tanyard, the houses that I own on Rooks Creek, and all my land. Further — they will have half my gold, the other half of which I give to Mary-Jane and Susan.

Susan Here it is, Uncle Harvey — six thousand dollars, and half of it is yours.

Gasps. The King nearly faints. The Duke cannot contain himself

Duke *Yes!*

Horrified pause. The Duke converts his "Yes!" into a series of sneezes. The King covers for him

King Poor creature! So happy — he forgets his affliction.

An eruption of cheers, tears and jollity

   Robinson stalks away

   The King and the Duke are escorted from the room clutching the gold

Scene 17

The Tunnel

Huck is left in the room

Huck That night I were kinda restless. Thinking o' Jim, and those two girls, and how those frauds were going to rob them of their money. I crep' downstairs 'n come to the parlour where old Peter Wilks were lying ...

A trapdoor opens smartly and startlingly by his feet. He jumps a mile in the air, then backs off

Susan clambers up out of the trap with lamp and empty bag. She shuts the trap, turns and sees Huck. Screams. Recovers

Susan Adolphus! Ain't you gone to bed?
Huck No ma'am. I couldn't sleep.
Susan (*flustered*) Poor boy. So far from home. Here, sit down a moment. Talk to me. Tell me about England — that will make you feel a little better.
Huck No! — Well, yes — but — sure it ain't so diff'rent. (*Pointing at the trap*) Miss Susan, please, tell me. What was you doing there when I first saw you?
Susan Mary-Jane will not forgive me.
Huck I won't say a word.
Susan (*after a beat*) That trap leads to a tunnel and Sherburn's dungeon.

Uncle Peter led a dozen slaves to liberty — and Sherburn never found how
they escaped.

Huck (*excitedly*) And you?

Susan Oh no, Adolphus. Uncle Peter never told us how he smuggled them
away. Tonight I took the poor slave locked in Sherburn's dungeon there
some food and drink.

Huck *Jim*!

Susan What?

Huck By Jiminy! I love you for it! What a scheme!

Suddenly Mary-Jane calls out

Mary-Jane (*off*) Susan! Are you there?

Susan I'm coming, Mary-Jane! (*Nervous, to Huck*) I must go. I beg you —
don't betray me. Don't — whatever you do — tell Mary-Jane.

Mary-Jane (*off*) Susan!

Susan Good-night. God bless you — you sweet boy.

She kisses him lightly and goes

Huck (*to us*) Well, what would you a done? Gone back to bed? Not likely.
All at once I knew that I could save Jim, help those girls, git out from under
those two jackals, git back on the river ... Mebbe it was all a little muddy—
but I knew that it would come out clean. Oh Jim, I'm coming for you,
Honey.

And he opens the trap and dives through it

SCENE 18

A Deal

The cellar/dungeon of the Sherburn mansion

The flickering light of an old oil lamp

*Sherburn — mean and angry, Jim behind bars, Pike nervy, Tom Sawyer at
bay*

Jim (*astonished*) Tom Sawyer! What you doin' here?

Sherburn You want him back?

Tom I'm not prepared to sell, Colonel Sherburn. It was my dear aunt's final

wish that I should find him — and then bring him back to work her land
when she was gone.

Sherburn I haven't chased him half across America to lose him now. You'll
take this money boy, or I won't answer for the consequences.

Jim Doan put yoursel' in danger, Tom. Clear out! Dis man woan lis'n to no
reason.

Tom (*cool*) Well I defy him!

Sherburn (*very quiet*) A boy comes South to see his Aunt in Memphis. Stops
in a little town called Bricksville. Nobody knows why. They look for him
a little — but he don't show up. Pike here knows what happened to him,
though. You know Pike don't you?

Pike Mebbe.

Sherburn He played a game with him. You like that, don't you, Pike? He
played a game with him.

Pike An' how does this one end? Tell me that, Sherburn!

Sherburn Like all the others, Pike. You win. The boy here loses. Unless of
course he signs this bill of sale.

Tom *Never*!

And he tears it up

Sherburn Why — you little ... !

Sherburn knocks Tom to the floor

Suddenly — the trap in Sherburn's dungeon flies open

Huck I'll buy the slave. I'll buy him from you, Sherburn.

Sherburn What the devil!

Pike Where did you spring from?

Tom (*with real interest*) My Lord — a ghost! *A ghost!*

Jim Is you crazy, boy?

Huck I said I'd buy him from you, Sherburn ——

Sherburn Where did you come from?

Huck — for three thousand dollars!

Pike You're mad, boy. Three thousand dollars? Where would you git three
thousand dollars?

Huck Stolen it.

Sherburn Where from?

Huck From Wilks!

A big moment. Sherburn wasn't expecting this

Sherburn *Show me.*

Hucks leads Sherburn and Pike out, down the trap

Tom I'm proud of him.
Jim What's that?
Tom I really thought that he was dead. That's skilful, real skilful. He has a lot to learn of course — but he'll do well.
Jim We all three's got some tings to learn if we's ever goan t'see anudder day!
Tom How we going to get you out of here?
Jim Fetch down a crow-bar or a saw. I's git through these blame chains in no time. Then throo' dat tunnel an' away — wouldn't dat work?
Tom Work? Why certainly it would *work* — but it's too darn simple. There ain't nothing to it. What's the good of a plan that ain't no more trouble than that? We'll need a rope-ladder for the battlements, and something for the moat, and then a pie to put the file in. That's gaudy, Jim.

And he dashes out after Huck and Sherburn

I tink we got enuff trouble, Tom Sawyer, without you imaginating up some more!

SCENE 19

The Gold

The Wilks' parlour. The coffin. The darkness begins to lighten

The trap opens

Sherburn and Pike follow Huck out into the room

Sherburn (*hisses*) Where's the money, boy?
Huck Wait here. I'll fetch it.
Pike No tricks — no tricks, boy!
Sherburn He knows I've got the slave. He wouldn't risk it.
Huck That's right. That's right. I want Missouri Jim.
Sherburn Hurry!

Huck rushes out of the room

A beat. Sherburn looks at the coffin

Sherburn What the devil's that? (*He whisks away the cloth covering it*)
Damn me — the coffin. It's Wilks' body.

Pike gasps

Are you scared, Pike? Why is that I wonder? You've led so many to their
deaths. Does this old troublemaker frighten you? Or do you feel him at your
back — pulling you down? It's a deep pit, Pike — the guilty never lose sight
of it. And men like Wilks are always there to push you in. From beyond the
grave.

During the following Tom comes up through the trap

Sherburn pushes Pike's head into the coffin

Pike screams, dodges, turns and rushes into Tom

Pike screams again and disappears down into the tunnel

Tom Forgive me. Did I disturb you?

Huck reappears — clutching the bags of gold

Huck Here's the money — three thousand dollars for Jim's freedom.

*Sherburn opens the bag. If possible, a light from within the bag dimly
illuminates his face. Sherburn gasps*

Sherburn There must be six thousand dollars here at least. Six thousand
dollars. (*A beat*) And you want to give me half.
Huck It's double what you'd get in Baton Rouge, three times the price they'd
pay in Natchez.
Sherburn It's amusing. The thought of river urchins telling me their terms.
"Oh Colonel Sherburn you can have three thousand dollars and no more
— that's what we think the slave is worth." Suppose I told you he was worth
six thousand to me, suppose I told you he was worth ten thousand, suppose
I took this money here, and took the slave as well. What could you do, what
could you do?

*Suddenly—from outside the room, we hear the drone of a clergyman's voice:
Revelations 14, from about verse 10*

What the devil's that?

Tom I don't know.

Huck They're heading this way. Hide! Hide! Put the money in the coffin — nobody will touch it there.

Tom Quickly, quickly!

Huck Colonel Sherburn — hide under there. We'll soon get rid of them.

The door bursts open

Huck just gets the lid back on the coffin, and he, Tom and Sherburn get out of sight just in time

In walks Mary-Jane, Susan, the Duke, the King, Levi Bell and one other

Huck and Tom look on, horrified. Of course — it's the day of the funeral. The reading from Revelations fills the room

The four men pick up the coffin and move out with it

The girls weep and look brave. The door closes behind this little procession. Huck and Tom look in shock at the deserted trestles

Sherburn (*emerging, furious*) You stupid fools — it's gone! Six thousand dollars — gone.

Tom (*suddenly, loudly, despairingly*) All right, all right! You've won. You're cunninger, cleverer. You've got us beat. I'd not've thought of that. It's gaudy — yes — passin' audacious and impertinent. Why, Casanova would be proud of it.

Sherburn Damn you, boy — what do you mean?

Tom You got the gold away from us. (*Crying*) Oh my ——

Huck (*prompting*) Adolphus.

Tom Adolphus — what shall we do — he's taken all poor Peter Wilks' money — put it in the cemetery. And then tonight — why he'll go there with a pick-axe and a shovel and he'll dig it out — while we sit helpless here. And what can we do?

Sherburn What indeed? And if you ever breath a word of this ... Open the trap.

Huck does

Good-morning, gentlemen. And please remember. Your silence or your lives.

And he goes

Tom springs up, cheerfully

Tom Good!
Huck What?
Tom You take your hat off to me.
Huck Why Tom Sawyer — what you hatchin' now?
Tom We'll watch for him tonight. The moment that he's gone — his house
is ours. We know the secret passage in — though now I have to say that
seems a little easy for my taste. By this time tomorrow, Jim will be a free
man — and history will crown us worthy sucessors to the Abbe Farria, who
dug the prisoner from the Castle Deef. Why this is fine, Huck.
Huck ⎫
Tom ⎬ *(together) Fox — Wolf — Bear!*
Tom I'm kinda glad I made the journey! Tell me everything. I want to know.

SCENE 20

The Wake

A sudden change of atmosphere. Later in the day. Sound of party hubbub

The mourners enter — eating corn pone and drinking punch

King Of course — now that poor Peter is in his grave — we must all look
to the future. Life is for the living. The dead pass on. For you know that
Joshua and Caleb lived still and went into the land of the Amedlikites, and
the Missourilates. Pass me the jug of punch, my dear.
Mary-Jane We would not have survived these troubled days without you,
Uncle Harvey. You have been a strong pillar to this house.
Susan Amen.
King We must soon return to England.
Mary-Jane ⎫
Susan   ⎬ *(together)* No!
King But you will come with us! Yes — you will accompany your uncles
to a new life across the ocean. Fill up this cup — dear, dear Mary-Jane.
Susan It's what we'd hoped and prayed for — to see England and the King.
King Ah — sweet King George.
Huck *(hissing)* William!
King William!
Doctor *(sharply)* Queen Victoria.
King Yes, yes — his lovely wife.
Susan And Sheffield!
King Ah, Sheffield, Sheffield — God bless Sheffield. Ah, the palace, and

the great zoo, the parks, the hanging gardens. And the great cathedral. The cathedral of Sheffield with its leaning tower.

The Duke bangs the table as a warning

Susan It sounds sublime. Oh, Uncle Harvey, Uncle William. I can hardly wait.

Much hugging and kissing — interrupted by a sudden knock at the door

King Adolphus! See to that ... Now let me see — I think we all should travel First Class on the journey back. The biggest suite a'rooms they got ...

The door opens to reveal two strangers, one of whom looks remarkably like Peter Wilks

Harvey (*authentic Yorkshire accent*) Good-evening to you all. I hear we have arrived too late.
King (*expansively*) No, no — You're not a bit late, whoever y'are — there's plen'y punch and corn-pone left!
Harvey Thank you indeed. We are a little hungry. It's many hours since we ate. My brother and I have had misfortunes: our baggage got put off at a town above here by mistake.
King Well that's too bad, ole man — these blame steam-ship companies. Unreliant, unreliant! Come in, sit down, drink up!
Harvey That's very kind of you. Perhaps we should introduce ourselves. I am Peter Wilks' brother, Harvey; and this is his brother William, who can't hear or speak. When was the funeral?

Everybody stops still. The King alone parties on

King Good, good, you're welcome, very, very welcome. Now let me see, let me see. I'll introduce you. Well then — this over here (*pointing at the Duke*) is Peter's brother William — who is just deef an' dumb, — and I'm — well I'm Harvey — Harvey Wilks — the elder brother — of the — er ... the elder brother of ... the ... who did you say you were?
Harvey I said. I am Peter Wilks' brother Harvey. And this is his brother, William.

A longish beat

King (*raising his eyes to Heaven*) To think that there should be such rogues and rascals in the world. It's hardly to be thought on. Dear Peter only lately

in his grave and two imposters come to discompose the solemn mourning
of the house. Oh, Mary-Jane, oh, Susan — shut your ears to their
fraudacious duperies ——

Harvey We are who we say we are! And in a day or two, when I get the
baggage, I can prove it.

King When he gets his baggage! That's mighty good! And mighty ingenious
— under the circumstances!

Harvey But it's true!

Doctor (*grimly*) I think we should look into this.

*Everybody except Huck draws off into a group. We hear a hubbub through
the next speech*

Huck turns to the audience

Huck Well — they sailed in on a general investigation. And there we had
it, up and down, hour in, hour out — and it was the worst mix-up thing you
ever see. They made the King tell his yarn, and they made the old
gentleman tell his, and anybody but a lot of prejudiced chuckleheads would
a seen that the new old gentleman was spinning truth, and t'other one lies.

The group breaks DS. *Very different moods this time. Girls crying. King edgy,
Harvey resolute*

Doctor (*pointing at the King and Duke*) It's my belief that these men are the
frauds. But if they ain't — they won't object to sending for that money —
the six thousand dollars in gold that Mary-Jane there gave them — and
letting us keep it till they prove they're all right. Ain't that so?

General agreement

King Well, that'll be my pleasure, gentlemen. (*Turning to the Duke*) William
— (*making nonsensical signs*) go and bring the gold. You know where we
hid it.

And the Duke flies out of the room

We'll do any darn thing you ask of us, to prove we is the rightful brothers
of poor Peter. Why, it must make his poor body tremble in its winding sheet
to hear these villains question our veraciousness.

Suddenly, there is a great cry — a strangled sort of howl. Everyone freezes

The Duke staggers back into the room

Duke Sgoo — Sgoo — sgon — sgone — snotthere — sgoo, sgoo — sgo sgone — sgo — sgoo — goo — goo

The King slaps him. Silence. The King turns slowly. All eyes are on him

King (*in a tiny vioce*) It's bin stolen.
Doctor *What?*
King It's gone. We hid it in the mattress. But it's gone.
Doctor (*exploding*) You rogues, you rapscallions, you lyin', cheatin', fraudulating villains!
Huck (*suddenly*) But Mister Wilks, sir. Don't you recall? (*A beat*) You told me that you weren't such a one for earthly riches and such like, and that the money was poor Peter's an' that no-one else should have it. Even in death.
King I did?
Huck An' then I helped you carry it downstairs an' give it back to him.
Doctor What do you mean, boy?
Huck Why sir — we put it in the coffin.
Doctor What?
Huck We put it in the coffin. With the body.

All (*outburst*)

Humbug and hogwash!
He's in league with them.
He's such a nice boy.
Adolphus, is that true?
I knew these men weren't lying.
What saints!
Where's the coffin now?
Of course it's true.

Doctor (*loudly*) There's only one way we can settle this. Come. Get your lights and lanterns. We'll dig up the coffin and look.
Harvey And when we do — we'll take a look and see what was tattooed on brother Peter's breast.
Doctor What's that?
Harvey Perhaps this gentleman can tell us what it is.

All eyes on the King. a tense moment

King (*cool as a frame of cucumbers*) Hmf! It's a very tough question, ain't it! Yes, sir, I c'n tell you what's tattooed on his breast. It's jest a small thin blue arrow — that's what it is. Now what do you say — hey?
Harvey I say that on his breast was a small dim P, and a B and a W — with dashes all between them. That's what I say.

King Does you indeed.

Harvey I do.

Doctor Collar all these four, and bring them to the graveyard. We'll find out the truth *tonight*!

They all exit, leaving Huck alone on stage

SCENE 21

The Great Escape

Huck I reckoned we had two hours. Just two hours.

Tom (*rushing in*) Sherburn left half an hour back. Just as we planned. It's goin' dandy.

Huck He's goin' to git an awful big surprise.

Tom For sure — the gold.

Huck Nope. Half the town is headin' for the graveyard.

Tom (*way ahead*) The real brothers showed?

Huck You bet they did.

Tom A brilliant twist! Now — our plan. We must do this thing according to the *rules*. I've got a disguise for Jim, the rope ladder for the battlements and a pen of course — so Jim can leave some messages behind him ...

Huck We better shift us! C'mon, let's move.

Huck and Tom exit

SCENE 22

Scene The Last

A huge commotion. The party from the graveyard pile back into the room — bearing before them Sherburn, the Duke and the King. [With a cast of ten, William has failed to make the return journey and appears now as Judge Levi Bell]

Mary-Jane Which is the worst of these atrocious villains?

Susan The devil who would rob the man he murdered?

Harvey Or the rogues who masqueraded as his brothers?

King Or the cottonheads who fell for it?

Bell Be quiet! Colonel Sherburn. What do you have to say?

Sherburn Nothing.

Bell I urge you to speak out. You stand in danger of the gravest accusations. How did you know the gold was in the coffin? What did you intend?

Sherburn I was cheated — swindled by a pair of boys. That money's mine. They gave it to me.

Mary-Jane Who?

Susan Adolphus? No — surely not!

Sherburn They gave it to me for a slave. They told me it was in the coffin.

King That young *scoundrel* — scamp. I'll leather him. This time he's brought us into trouble.

Bell Send out to find the boy!

Duke Where is the wretch?

Harvey There's maybe something he can tell us.

Susan I think perhaps there is ...

And suddenly the trap flies open: Tom, Jim and Huck climb out, unaware of the crowd behind them in the room

Tom Huck! One night lets we three slide on out a'here and get an outfit — then go for howlin' adventures 'mongst the injuns. Just for a week or two.

Huck Well, let's get out of here first!

They turn — mid-whoop — and suddenly see who's in the room

I'm sorry!

Tom Wrong room!

Jim So sorry ...

And they head for the trap

Bell Stop right there!

Tom Oh my.

Jim Dis poor body jus' can't have no luck. Dis is de end for us.

Sherburn (*a yelp of rage*) Judge Bell! You're looking for a villain — there he is. That boy there stole the money from this house — pretended it was his to use, wanted to buy that slave. This other boy — *claimed* that he owned him, *claimed* to be the nephew of the woman that I tried to buy him from. Both liars and thieves. And as for these two (*pointing to the King and the Duke*) — they were in league to help this runaway. Arrest the slave! Arrest these boys and lock them up! Arrest these two for aiding and consorting with a runaway. And lastly: ask these ladies what they might know about a secret passage to my house, a secret passage shown me by these boys — through which for ten years they and their Uncle smuggled out my slaves and set them free! *All guilty — guilty!*

A terrible silence. Then — a small cough

Tom Allow me to introduce myself. My name's Tom Sawyer. I'm on my way from Petersburg to Memphis, where my aunt lives. I'm an old friend of Huckleberry here.

All Huckleberry?

Tom His real name is Huckleberry Finn. And hearing you just now reminded me — I have a letter.

All (*together*)
- A letter?
- What letter?
- How can a letter help?
- What's he blethering about?

Tom Miss Watson — the owner of this slave until her death — gave me a letter which may help to clear this whole affair. Judge Bell — perhaps you'll read it.

Bell Have *you* read it, boy?

Tom She made me swear that I wouldn't. Here it is.

Everyone gathers round

Bell Well this is most extraordinary! These papers — signed by Miss Watson, and counter-signed by the Governor of Missouri, Meredith M. Marmaduke — grant absolute freedom to the loved and misused Jim — her slave for fifteen years.

Gasps

Huck Jim!

Jim Oh my lordy!

Bell And further — she has left sufficient money in her will to purchase his wife and children, and begs forgiveness from her former slave for ever parting them.

Susan Oh what a hard bad world it is.

Mary-Jane Amen.

Bell So, Colonel Sherburn. The situation seems a little different now. This man was free when you abducted him. These men were quite entitled to consort with him. This boy here certainly had an acquaintance with Miss Watson. I guess this other boy — took the money from these frauds and tried to do some good with it. So. Jim ain't yours, and neither is the money.

A beat

Sherburn I'll go.

Tom Colonel Sherburn! I don't suppose you ever noticed — but prisoners *do* write on walls.

Bell What's that?

Tom In your dungeon there, half a dozen made their mark. All prisoners — unjustly held: free men — kidnapped illegally.

Sherburn It's not illegal *here*.

Susan But one day *soon* ...

Mary-Jane You know what's legal — but we know what's *right*. Your ways are an abomination. You poison the sweet air from heaven.

Bell (*to Sherburn*) You'd better go.

Susan And may the souls of your poor victims' haunt you to the day you die.

Mary-Jane Amen.

Sherburn moves slowly to the door

Sherburn This ain't a world for men — only idiots and women.

He stalks away

A silence. Shock, relief

Bell (*to the Duke and the King*) But as for you two ——

Duke *Deeply wronged!*

Bell What's that?

Duke Maligned and slandered.

Bell How?

Duke I have been this boy's protector, I have been this man's deliverer!

King Snatched him from the jaws of death, fed them when we was hungry!

Duke *In extremis* — undertook a desperate endeavour; forsook our true identities, assumed a low disguise.

King Stooped to deception! Pretended we was no-goods ...

Duke We helped a child and a fugitive! What other course was open to us? What man of stone would not have plucked these howling wretches from the torrent? What have we dared, what have we risked?

King (*appealing to the audience*) Folks say — give 'em a reward! These two deserve no less! I've heard 'em say five hundred! I've heard 'em say a thousand!

A beat

Duke We'll settle for a hundred each ...

King Or split between the two of us!

Duke Forty?

King Thirty, perhaps?

Duke Ten each and expenses?

Bell I should flog you both within an inch of your mis'rable lives!

The Duke and the King kneel

King (*after a very slight beat*) Two inches?
Duke Three?
Bell *Be quiet!* Scoundrels! Liars and cheats!
Duke But we are only *sometimes* what you say we are. Days have passed when we have scarcely lied or cheated once; weeks at a time have found us virtuous.
Harvey And which of us can claim more than that, Judge Bell. For my part, I forgive them. While men like Sherburn live within the law, you need a pair like this to make a fool of it.
Mary-Jane Amen!
Duke ⎱
King ⎰ (*together*) Amen!
Bell Well — in that case, perhaps you'd like to take them back with you to Sheffield, Mister Wilks?
Harvey Ay — they'd prosper there!

The Duke and the King sink to their knees, truly horrified

Duke Not Sheffield!
King *No*!
Bell The sentence is passed! Sheffield it is!
All Hooray!
Duke This is worse than a flogging ...
Susan Come — let's raise a glass.

Music starts

Drinks are poured

To our new found Uncles, to Jim's liberty, to Sherburn's ruin, and — to this child — Adolphus ...
Mary-Jane Sarah Williams ——
Harvey John Peters ——
King George Jackson ——
Jim Huckleberry Finn!
All *Huckleberry Finn*!
Susan You're welcome here. Stay with us. This could be your home.
Harvey I second that. You can be one of the family.
Mary-Jane Oh, say you will.

Bell That's quite enough! Leave the poor boy alone and *take your partners*! Miss Susan, Miss Mary-Jane ... Lead away!

And the Company barn-dance. Near the end, they freeze: the music stops, the Lights focus on Huck, who turns to the audience

Huck Well — I reckon I got to light out for the Territory ahead of the rest, because this Susan Wilks seems all set to adopt me and civilize me, and I can't stand it. (*A beat*) I been there before.

And he rejoins the dance, which reaches a rousing climax and a deep bow

FURNITURE AND PROPERTY LIST

Only the furniture and properties mentioned in the text are listed here. Further items
may be added at the director's discretion

ACT I

On stage: HUCK'S BEDROOM
Big, uncomfortable old bed. *On it*: crisp bedclothes
Stick
Coats on the wall
Books
PAP'S CABIN
Straw mattress. *On it*: blankets
Stove
Barrel
Whiskey bottles
JUDITH'S KITCHEN
Dresser. *On it*: spectacles
Two stones
Needle and thread
Bin
Rat
GENERAL
Canoe
Stick with snake attached
Gun
Catfish
Fishing rod
Boxes
Bundles
Raft
Pole
GRANGERFORDS
Furniture
Glasses with drinks, food
Cards

Off stage: Lamp (**Miss Watson**)
Noose (**Stage Management**)
Vanity bag (**Sophia**)
Portmanteau (**Sophia**)

                Carpet bag (**Sophia**)
                Guns and weapons (**Grangerfords**)

Personal: **Blackhat 1 (Pap)**: knife
                Charlotte: cheroot
                Tom: dollar coin
                Bob: clasp knife

INTERVAL PROLOGUE

Off stage: Temperance banner (**The King**)
                Bag (**The King**)
                Chair (**The Duke**)
                Case. *In it*: props (**The Duke**)
                Torches/Lanterns (**Townspeople**)

ACT II

Off stage: Gun (**Wilks**)
                Gun (**Sherburn**)
                Arms (**Sherburn**)
                Arms (**Pike**)
                Dungeon chains (**Stage Management**)
                Trestles. *On them*: coffin (**Stage Management**)
                Wilks's parlour table. *On it*: drinks (**Stage Management**)
                Book of scriptures (**Mary-Jane**)
                Bag of gold (**The Duke**)
                Lamp (**Susan**)
                Empty bag (**Susan**)
                Bible (**Clergyman**)
                Corn-pone (**Mourners**)
                Glasses of punch (**Mourners**)

LIGHTING PLOT

Practical fittings required: lamp for Miss Watson and the Widow
Property fittings required: none
Various interior and exterior settings

ACT I

To open: When **Huck** wakes snap up general shadow effect

Cue 1	**Jim** slips away *Effect of shadows dancing and stirring*	(Page 1)
Cue 2	**Miss Watson** and the **Widow Douglas** enter *Dim lighting with cover spot for* **Miss Watson** *and* **Widow**	(Page 3)
Cue 3	**Miss Watson** and the **Widow** exit *Cut cover spot. Bring up dark and shadowy lighting, moonlight effect through the window*	(Page 4)
Cue 4	To open Scene 4 *Lights suggest violent abduction*	(Page 9)
Cue 5	**Huck** lies down to sleep *Bring up daylight effect*	(Page 12)
Cue 6	**Huck**: "…the canoe from the outside." *Evening river effect*	(Page 14)
Cue 7	**Jim**: "… wid de ole missus …" *Cross-fade to Widow's room*	(Page 16)
Cue 8	**Miss Watson**: "… and bring your gold!" *Cross-fade to Jim and Huck on the raft*	(Page 16)
Cue 9	**Jim** and **Huck** fall back laughing *Cross-fade to the Widow's room*	(Page 17)
Cue 10	**Pike**: "Way beyond the law …" *Cross-fade to island setting*	(Page 17)
Cue 11	**Huck** races away *Bring up spot on Pike*	(Page 18)

INTERVAL PROLOGUE

ACT II

Cue 26	**The King** and **The Duke** sing and snore *When ready, bring up sunset effect*	(Page 58)
Cue 27	**Mary-Jane** screams and runs to **Wilks's** body *Bring up spot on* **Huck**	(Page 58)
Cue 28	**Huck**: "For one night only!" *Fade spot on* **Huck**, *bring up general lighting*	(Page 59)
Cue 29	**Jim**: " … come to *marryin'*." *Flickering torch effect*	(Page 60)
Cue 30	To open Scene 12 *Bring up old-fashioned playhouse lighting*	(Page 61)
Cue 31	**Sherburn** fires his gun *Black-out*	(Page 63)
Cue 32	When ready *Lights up on tableau*	(Page 64)
Cue 33	To open Scene 14 *General lighting*	(Page 64)
Cue 34	**Duke**: "The future calls!" *Cross-fade to dungeon* us	(Page 65)
Cue 35	**Huck**: "… I'd never find another." *Dark street effect*	(Page 65)
Cue 36	**Tom**: "… travelling in your direction." *Cross-fade to* **Wilks's** *parlour*	(Page 66)
Cue 37	To open Scene 18 *Cross-fade to dungeon. Flicker of old oil lamp*	(Page 71)
Cue 38	**Jim**: "… imaginating up some more!" *Cross-fade gradually to* **Wilk's** *parlour*	(Page 73)
Cue 39	**Huck**: " — three thousand dollars for Jim's freedom." *Light effect from bag of gold, illuminating* **Sherburn**'s *face*	(Page 74)
Cue 40	**Bell**: "Lead away!" *After music stops, lights focus on* **Huck**	(Page 85)
Cue 41	**Huck**: "I been there before." *Bring up general lighting*	(Page 85)

EFFECTS PLOT

ACT I

Cue 1   **Miss Watson**: " ... I'll deal with him in the morning."   (Page 4)
Outside night noises effect

Cue 2   **Huck**: "Your gang?"   (Page 6)
Sudden knock at the door

Cue 3   **Pap**: "... to be a family once again."   (Page 9)
Music

Cue 4   **Pap**: "... kill you ..."   (Page 12)
A note of music

Cue 5   **Huck** lies down to sleep   (Page 12)
A cock crows

Cue 6   **Pap** stumbles out   (Page 12)
Sound of door locking. Music

Cue 7   **Voice**: "Take care! Don't miss!"   (Page 13)
Sound of a shot

Cue 8   **All**: *"The canoe!"*   (Page 13)
Music bursts out

Cue 9   **Huck**: "And I'll be free. *Free!*"   (Page 13)
The music swells

Cue 10   **Huck**: "... canoe from the outside."   (Page 14)
Evening on the river, echoey sounds

Cue 11   **Voice 2**: "But another man twice as well ..."   (Page 14)
A loud echoey boom sound

Cue 12   **Huck**: "... make my carcass come to the top —-"   (Page 14)
Another loud boom

Cue 13   **Miss Watson**: "— if the good Lord will have him ..."   (Page 14)
Boom sound

Cue 14   **Jim:** "I tink I could!"   (Page 17)
              Music

Cue 15   **Judith:** "… bringin' me here."   (Page 19)
              Knock at the door

Cue 16   **Judith** picks up the rat   (Page 21)
              Sound of rat squeaking

Cue 17 .   **Jim:** "Huck — push her away!"   (Page 23)
              Big river music, mist under raft, music to underscore

Cue 18   **Huck:** "… the whole world lit up."   (Page 23)
              "World lit up" sound effect

Cue 19   **Pike:** "Is your man black or white?   (Page 25)
              Music

Cue 20   **The Widow** and **Miss Watson** melt away   (Page 26)
              Music stops

Cue 21   **Huck:** "On the fifth night after this ——"   (Page 27)
              *Thunder effect, rain, sound of steamboat's horn, drone
              of steamboat approaching commences, gradual
              crescendo, crash of wood on wood, etc.*

Cue 22   **Jim** and **Huck** are separated   (Page 27)
              Sound of boat dies away, rain continues

Cue 23   **Huck** sinks to his knees   (Page 28)
              Rain stops

Cue 24   **Huck:** "Hello!"   (Page 28)
              Wild burst of barking

Cue 25   **Children:** " 'We'd keep the devil in line!'"   (Page 33)
              Music

Cue 26   Members of the family dance   (Page 33)
              Sudden burst of rifle shots

Cue 27   **Sophia** drives away with **Huck**   (Page 37)
              Sound of carriage wheels

Cue 28   **Jim:** "In de hotel wid a young lady …"   (Page 38)
              Music

INTERVAL PROLOGUE

ACT II

Cue 43   **Susan**: "Come — let's raise a glass."   (Page 84)
              Music starts

Cue 44   The **Company** freeze   (Page 85)
              Music stops

Cue 45   **Huck**: "I been there before."   (Page 85)
              Music continues